Dialogue on Awakening

Communion With A Loving Brother

By Tom and Linda Carpenter

DIALOGUE ON AWAKENING

ISBN 978-0-9633051-4-5

1992: Original Printing:
Dialogue on Awakening: Communion with a Loving Brother

Other material from Tom Carpenter:
Book: "*The Miracle of Real Forgiveness: Freeing us to Love*", 2010
DVD: "*A Dialogue on Forgiveness*" with Robert Holden, PhD

Books and DVD available from Amazon.com
Or directly from:
www.TomAndLindaCarpenter.com

For more of Tom's awareness, also see:
Facebook.com/TheForgivenessNetwork
www.TheForgivenessMovement.org

"There is nothing that happens to you; there are only the thought processes and patterns of the state of mind in which you exist...What you experience as your physical reality is only a confirmation of what you are experiencing in your mind."

Pg 73

"There is only one thing to remember and that is you are already awake ... you simply refuse to believe it. And it is in this refusal that you remain in the domain of limitations."

Pg 11

"The Love that is present within you is a wondrous thing to share. It is your sharing of this Love that is the most significant thing you do. Again, it becomes a matter of allowing the feeling to become the focus. Words can be received and misperceived, but they are at all times within the realm of perception. It is when you allow yourself to become fully immersed in the feeling of your Being, in the feeling of Love, that you will communicate to others who God Is... This will not happen with words."

Pg 148

All references to the "Course" refer to "A Course in Miracles" Dictated by the Christ Consciousness in communion with Helen Schucman. First introduced in 1976, it is considered by many to be one of the most profound teachings of our time. It is widely available online and in major bookstores, and has been translated into most major languages throughout the world.

Similar to the Course, when a word may refer to either an aspect of God or our normal usage, it is sometimes capitalized for clarity when referring to God's Creation.

Tom's use of the male pronouns are merely common usage and do not truly reflect the abstract nature of God, which is beyond the duality of either male or female.

Contents

Note to Reader Regarding Questions and Answers

Initially, both Tom and I asked many questions of this beautiful Source who connected with Tom's mind. I soon began recording the answers Tom shared to save and study the information. Soon, other people began also asking for help or clarification, so we also recorded those dialogues. However, as much of the information given was meaningful to many of us, I began transcribing them to share with others. Eventually, we had a large collection of transcripts that we later put together as this book, and the name, "Dialogue on Awakening", seemed appropriate.

When you read a question, it is from someone who asked "Brother" through Tom for information or help. When there is no question, you are reading information Tom was inquiring about and which he wrote down as it was given.

Linda Carpenter

Introduction

Messages

"Expanded consciousness literally has no room for that which does not wholly embrace the loving harmony of all things."

What is Awakening?

"Awakening" is a word that refers to the experience of remembering that we are created in the image and likeness of the Essence of God: perfect, eternal, unified and unchangeable; that our real or true essence is eternal Spirit rather than our temporary human form. Great teachers such as Jesus, Buddha and many others have quietly within their mind awakened to a great degree of this reality while still in physical form. It is the purpose of these dialogues with the Christ consciousness to help us realize it is inevitable that we all will eventually make choices leading to the same Awakening.

In these dialogues, we are told that the changing world of form and imperfect bodies where we experience the duality of both love and fear, pleasure and suffering, birth, death, and many other experiences, is not the Creation of God. The human experience is of our own making. It is based upon a mistaken belief that it is possible to be separate from the pure harmony and Love of the one unified Mind of God and, therefore, from each other and from all other life. Because we are eternally the Essence of our Creator as Spirit, we are so powerful that whatever we choose to focus on in our mind must become our experience. Therefore, the world we now appear to "see" is simply a mirror for how mentally we perceive ourselves The purpose of the information in this book is to help us change how we see ourselves..

Because being Awakened is our pre-existent state of Being, there is nothing to earn, to learn, or to do to return to it but to release our mistaken perceptions of separation. As we remember who we truly are, we Awaken as if from a dream; discovering that all that we have experienced here in this realm of polarities, seemingly apart from the harmony of Creation, has had no effect whatsoever on our own eternal perfection of God.

It is the experience of realizing who we truly are that Jesus discovered and began teaching over two thousand years ago, and continues more completely in these dialogues today.

Linda Carpenter

An Introduction
By Tom Carpenter

My experience of mentally communicating with Brother, as I call this "inner voice," began with conflicting emotions. Mixed with doubt was a sense of excitement and wonder at the prospects of what appeared to be an extraordinary adventure. The possibilities for satisfying my highly curious mind seemed endless as there was no question I could ask that was not immediately answered. It was like having an encyclopedia of universal knowledge available at my request.

After a short period of time, however, as the superficial fascination was wearing off, I came face to face with my logical mind wanting to reject the entire experience. It became a roller coaster with wonderful feelings during the course of a "conversation," being followed by the absolute conviction that it was only my imagination running rampant. Finally, I insisted on some physical proof to satisfy my doubting mind. I received my proof, of course, but not by way of some physical manipulation. The birth of my grandson was instead revealed to me in such a way that left no room for doubt.

My learning experience after that seemed at various times to take many directional shifts. Looking back, however, I can see there was a very steady course being taken, with his suggestions to shift my focus coming only when I was ready to take the next step.

About a year after our experience together had begun, Brother suggested that I begin to take more responsibility for the message I had felt was coming strictly from his awareness. He explained that by attributing the experience solely to him I was denying my ability to transcend the ego's limitations and find the place of knowing we all share. He said that where I joined with him and accepted his knowing was where I also would find my own knowing as well. I didn't realize it then, but he was introducing me to my God Self.

I asked if this meant that our time together was coming to a close. I felt his reassurance as he told me that now that I had accepted him it was no longer possible for us to be apart. I then remembered one of the very first things he had told me. I had asked why I felt drawn to call him "Brother," not Jesus. He said the feeling of being a brother made him more approachable. "But," he said, "the purpose for our being together is for you to feel equally comfortable knowing me as part of your Self."

A short time later we attended a gathering where I was expected to "channel" him. I had no idea of what to expect because of the earlier conversation. I went through the quieting process I used, mentally seeing him seated on a bench in our garden. I sat in the grass at his feet looking into his eyes and waiting for the flow of communication to begin. He sat there smiling, but saying nothing. I said, "Brother, I don't know what to do." He then held out his hand and said, "It will be easier when you come sit beside me." This was the most overpowering and loving-beyond-description moment I have ever experienced.

Jesus' teaches us that God has placed the Presence of the Holy Spirit in our mind that we would have access to a Presence of truth, of peace and love we had forgotten. Discovering, with Jesus guidance, that I could largely circumvent the ego's perception and access a place of knowing in my mind gives real meaning to what he says. When he said, "Come sit beside me," it was an invitation to share what he had found and hopefully I can extend that sharing to anyone willing to have it.

When he said that the purpose for our being together was for me to recognize him as part of my Self, he summed-up the purpose for all our learning. He has said in many ways that the source of all our illusions is the misperceived thought that it is possible for us to be separate from our Source and from one another

Many of the most satisfying moments I have spent with our Brother have been without the need for any kind of verbal communication.

In fact, the real sense of peace and love we have shared gave me new meaning to what communication is really for. I have also learned that I can have these moments with anyone I choose. All I need do is think of them as I think of him. And as I do, it is inevitable that I feel coming from them what I have received from him. A beautiful example of his teaching that giving and receiving are the same.

Jesus has said that our defenses against one another cause us more anxiety and unhappiness than we can possibly imagine. These are the defenses provoked by the belief that there is something wrong with us. We believe that we are deserving of attack and so look for it everywhere. Experiences of joining, whatever their form, teach us our defenses are unwarranted. My experience of joining with him has been a wonderful example of what we can expect when we let our defenses down and come together.

As strange as I had once felt about hearing a voice in my mind that seemed to have no logically identifiable source, I now know this inner communication to be a completely natural occurrence. There is nothing special about it. We all do it constantly, but because it doesn't follow the familiar pattern we associate with being a body it goes by unnoticed.

I must also emphasize, however, it is not the words that are most important. They too are only necessary between bodies. They are, in fact, not even how we now communicate. It is our intention for the words that communicates their meaning. When we pay attention we are aware when the messages we receive and give have little to do with the words we speak.

The significant importance of this kind of communication is recognizing and feeling of the presence of those you cannot identify with a physical form. We are not bodies in a finite place we call a world. We are beings of spirit communicating with our thoughts. Coming together, letting go the feeling we are separate, as we have said, is the most important element in our learning, and bodies cannot join. Beginning to recognize that our real "substance" is spirit is necessary to have any real appreciation for the infinite nature of who we are.

The experience of communion with our loving Brother has dramatically changed my beliefs about what is real and what is not so important. I now can see that the "wisdom" that will awaken the universe is about forgiveness, undoing the judgments we use to defend ourselves and stay separate from one another, not a greater understanding of how the world works or how to change it to be more acceptable to the ego's needs.

I still wonder why I continue to struggle with my daily ego concepts when I have tasted what it is like to be in that wonderfully peaceful state of mind. I still find it easy to be self-critical and judgmental about not staying in that "space." Then I remember when early in our relationship, I complained to Brother about my lack of ability to maintain my peace. He listened patiently, then said, "Please remember, there are only two choices you can ever make. You will either choose to experience the Peace of God, or you will choose something else. In which case, there is nothing happening."

We have no excuses to judge. We have either chosen to accept the Vision the Holy Spirit keeps for us, or become lost in the story of sin and separation. The ego is determined there will be a million paths to hell, with heaven just a dream. But it is just the opposite that is true. One simple truth will replace all despair: We cannot change what God has created like Himself. Just beyond all thoughts of pain and death, we live in perfect harmony with All That Is. This is forever true.

Blessings,

Tom Carpenter

An Introduction From Jesus as The Christ

There is much being said about the role of time in your Awakening process. It is felt by some that there are events occurring and preordained that will facilitate your shifting into a higher or greater state of conscious awareness. It is my suggestion that you do not regard the information I have presented herein from that perspective. See it simply as being in response to your request, your choice to remember your Divine nature.

When time is seen as a device capable of exerting any influence over you, you may be sure it is a self-imposed restriction for time was born with your mistaken belief that you had separated yourself from the Mind of God. Time is only the measurement of a dream that never was. It seems, however, to be the idea from which you extract the meaning of what you describe as the current moment or now. What you are seeking to understand as the "now" moment is not of time, for it has no measurement, no dimension. It is always present, it can neither pass nor be extended for it expresses the nature of who you are; it is infinite.

Your choice to remember will occur in the infinite present, as did your seeming choice to forget. They are the same moment, and it is because of this that you may rest assured you have never been disconnected from your loving Source. It is but a fleeting and humorous thought, impossible to be lodged in an idea of time that never was.

My encouragement to you will always be to merely let go of the ideas that convey a meaning that is not consistent with the always loving Reality of God, to let go of those ideas that are not congruent with your being the expression of His Reality.

I will always respond to your requests for information of any kind, but I must additionally say to you it will not be in accumulating this knowledge that you will find the wisdom you seek.

Expanded consciousness literally has no room for that which does not wholly embrace the loving harmony of all things. The whole Mind hears each note clear, yet blended perfectly to orchestrate the symphony of Creation. It is not possible for it to be otherwise for that would be a contradiction of who you are. What else could be involved then in your remembering but to let go of the idea that fear is real, holding God's Son prisoner within a dream. And who could cast your shackles off and throw wide the dungeon door of a nightmare never real? The dreamer and the dream are one. It is but you who must decide to wake. And you will choose the time, while it still seems to govern you.

Do this in peace, with no thought of fearful consequence for choice not made or wrongfully made. Look not to motivations born of fear. Remember instead that you are in this infinitely present moment, safely held in the loving embrace of your Creator. Accept completely this single thought and the idea of fear will vanish, its meaning now exposed. Your dream will now be done

Tom Carpenter
As the Following Message Began

I had become aware that for some time I had been very "discriminating" about books and articles I was reading, information from other channels and of attitudes and procedures employed by some who are teaching *A Course in Miracles.* I would examine the material to see if it fit within the parameters of the information I was receiving in order to evaluate the truth. And naturally, the more I focused on the differences, the more frequently I was confronted with them.

I was turning over in my mind the latest apparent conflict when I became aware of Jesus' presence and heard him ask if I would take a moment to review a mental picture he would give. This picture was an overview of the process leading to the formulation of our Bible.

In this mental picture, I saw various groups assigned to gather and sort through writings, both old and new, to choose which "Holy" words would eventually be considered the truth. This process created a great deal of dissension as everyone involved had strong opinions and loyalties to the material they considered most sacred. Eventually the edited materials were submitted to an "Executive Committee" who made the final decision on what was to be used. Here again, there was much discussion and disagreement over which words would best define the "Laws of God" for all time.

Yet from that time to the present, these "Holy" words have continued to be interpreted and reinterpreted to become the basis for a multitude of religions, each of which, in their zeal to promote and protect the most correct word of God, has mostly promoted the separation of themselves from their brothers. The meaning of "Love your brother as yourself" has become conditional on his believing words in the same way that you do.

As this picture unfolded, I found myself looking at my own recent experiences of judging what was "truth" passing up opportunities to see love expressing, and choosing instead to focus on the conflict the words presented. I became painfully aware that this was the same pattern repeated again. Then I heard Jesus gently ask, "Would you be willing to break this pattern?" I said yes, and he replied, "Then I would like your help in doing that."

I believe the following words are the beginning of this message.

A Message about Truth

It has long been man's obsession to seek for truth, to want to put a meaning to it, to have it for his own, to nurture and protect it, to make it the guiding beacon for his life. And in so doing, he has perhaps created the single thought that has most separated him from his brother. For you see, the truth is not in the word that you would hear another speak, or even in the thoughts he may have of himself as he holds that sense of self apart from you and from his Holy Father.

You would elevate me in the wisdom that you hope I bring because you believe that truth resides in me. Yet, I must tell you now, this is not truth. Truth is who I Am and truth is who you Are. When truth would lie within a word, you must feel a need to protect yourself from all those words that are not of truth and, therefore, hold yourself above the feeling of truth which is in the one who brings you the Presence of God. Can you not now see that through these many years as you have believed one truth about me and another would accept something different, that it has served a purpose only of holding you apart from him?

I will tell you now, if you will know truth and you will know it from its Source, then take the hand of the one who is next to you, hold it firm, and feel the flow of love that comes from who he is. See beyond the blindness of his eyes and accept the truth that is within you both that acknowledges the Presence of God in this simple act. Be with him, not in what he says, but in the pure acknowledgment that he is the Holy Presence of who you are.

Have you felt truth in moments of joy? For if you have not, you have missed its meaning. Truth is not a feeling of what is right and what is wrong—these are but judgments made of man. Truth is in the joy that releases you from fear. Truth is the presence of laughter as you feel the wind upon your face. Truth is every pure thought and feeling that reaches out to God and your brother. You will not find it in words.

Do you find peace as you would acknowledge the lack of truth you would hear a brother speak? Or does truth flow more simply as you look into the love you find in his eyes? You would say to me, but there are those into whose eyes I would look and see fear. And I must say to you, when you change the vision within yourself, you will see no fear. When truth is acknowledged as the Presence of who you Are, then truth will be present all around you.

Now, will you hear what I would say and believe it is my wisdom that would bring you truth? No, it may not be. But as you would sit quietly and know the truth within your mind, then you will touch me, and you will know the truth of who I Am. Do not elevate what I would have to say, but feel the meaning of my words. I come to you in love, for that is all I Am. I come to you as truth, for that is who you Are. And our joining will take place as this is accepted by you. Feel me within your heart—no closer and no farther away than the one who is next to you. Know that what I can bring you in this moment is only equal to what you would receive from him. You are the Holy Child of God; you are the Presence of His truth. Hold this clear that "truth" may be known for what it is and no longer misunderstood.

We are blessed for who we Are, and we bless the world when we see it being only the creation of our Holy Father. You are the blessing of all Creation and you bless It as It blesses you.

I am in peace and I would ask you to join me here.

Chapter One

Awakening

"What is it like to be enlightened or awake? It is when you see only God as cause, and effect being you expressing Him, wholly. You will no longer feel the need to see your mind as separately identified within the whole Mind, but you will feel its presence there and you will recognize your Self in it. Fear of any nature becomes unknown. Joy abounds with every thought as love is once again remembered."

What Being Awakened is Like

What is total enlightenment like? Are there degrees of illusion?

In the strictest meaning of what you are asking there is illusion and there is no illusion. The very concept of degrees is itself illusory. There are stages of your being aware of the illusion. To this extent you could refer to them as levels or whatever would fit as a descriptive term for you. But you know yourself as either asleep or Awake, and there is but a single idea which stands between the two. Dismiss the thought of separation from your mind and you will find yourself Home again. Remember only that your mind has never existed apart from the Mind of God. Accept wholly that your mind is a part of the Mind of God and that it is expressive of the whole Mind of God. There is nothing else you need concern yourself with. All other issues will naturally fade away as you accept this one thought.

Every doubt and contradiction that now plagues your mind is there because you do not experience your mind as being whole, connected to and interwoven with all Creation. You see instead a world fragmented, torn apart by different beings expressing different needs and desires, mostly in conflict with one another. You think because you see it performing this way that it must be real. You do not accept the truth that there is nothing out there that is not an extension of you because God's Son is not disconnected. This thought is too painful to accept as you think you witness the pain and hunger, brutality and fear that exists in your experience.

You see your world this way and believe that what you see is real, thereby transforming effect into cause. You believe yourself to be disconnected from the Mind of God for the same reason. You do not see it in your experience, therefore, it must not be true. Effect is again believed to be the cause.

Where does the healing of the world take place? When your mind again is seen as whole; the instant you look into a brother's eyes and see your Self reflected there. When your whole mind is known by you to mean every mind, all minds merged to One, the world will instantly change. It will be healed because you will see it to be so. You will have changed the cause by healing the thought of being separate from the Mind of God. The effect of then seeing only the world of God's perfection is instantaneous. With the misperceived thought now gone, cause and effect have become the same.

In your place of knowing, you resonate with the truth of what I am saying. Yet even now your ego will stand in dispute, asking how it could be possible for you to heal your mind and thereby heal all the world. On this denial have you laid the foundation for your belief in separation. It is from this belief all other misperceptions of truth seem verified. For it is from here you have become convinced that you are a product of the world's creation, subject to all its laws and influence. You believe you are the effect and not the cause.

What is it like to be enlightened or Awake? It is when you see only God as cause and effect being your expressing Him, wholly. You will no longer feel the need to see your mind as separately identified within the whole Mind, but you will feel its Presence there and you will recognize your Self in it. Fear of any nature becomes unknown. Joy abounds with every thought as Love is once again remembered.

The bonding that takes place that gels the mind as a whole is this Love. It is not an exclusive expression of love you experience within your state of limitation. Here is God expressed. And His Love makes no distinctions.

I have referred to a concept I describe as the power of One, the power that results from individual expressions of the infinite Mind as they come into recognition of their absolute unity—the infinite expression of wholeness, or One. It is this truth when fully grasped that will allow you to recognize your individuality in the whole, as the whole, expressing the whole and coincidentally being wholly, uniquely you.

Is this the state in which the Creator originally created us and we then believe we left to experience this separation?

The state of your Being remains forever unaltered. That is why it is easy for me to assure you that the reconnection you seek will come, and this quandary that seems to be overwhelming you at the moment will fall away. You have never changed. You are as the Father created you, but you just haven't let yourself remember it. You may also be very thankful that there is nothing you can do to change it. What could you fear if you kept repeating to yourself, "There is nothing I can do to alter my Being." Your mind is powerful enough to keep your attention from it, but it has absolutely no power to change it.

What happens to this limited mind when we return to our natural, unlimited state?

It does its natural thing; it extends itself. It expresses itself, it expresses the Self, and there is no difference. At this moment, you express yourself as being an identity that you see as being exclusive. But expressing your natural Self is an identity that sees no exclusivity; it simply expresses truth.

You will reach a point when truth Is. You are correct in your assumptions that truth is quite relative within the state of the dream. But beyond the dream you will recognize that it just Is. It will not have the connotations of being truth as it is expressed and described now, for this implies that there is something that is not truth. And, of course, when you are in a state of wholeness, there is nothing to which there is an opposite. And that is what you will express. It is at this point that you will understand your role as a creator because that is the essence of Creation. It is the extension of what I will now call the harmony of truth. I could call it Love . . . they are the same. They are the substance of your Being.

But you will not be lost, you will not dissolve within a common pot. Your identity, your true identity—and that is not a descriptive phrase as would be appropriate in reality, but I will use it here—your true identity is forever safely remembered and sacred in the Mind of God.

I know that you can be easily confused when I say you are me, and I am you, and we are One. That could lead you to believe that there is no recognition of your Self. What I am more appropriately trying to convey is that there is no difference in the recognition of our Selves and what we express and extend as the creative aspect of our Father. That becomes whole, that becomes totally unified and we express it together and there is no difference in our expression of it. Therein lies our unification and our wholeness. And there, too, lies your sacred individuality in its entire Divinity. You see, you have not dissolved or gone away.

Nothing is lost and you lose nothing here, hard as you may try. And nothing is happening while you are away because, as I keep repeating, you have never really gone.

For all concepts of wholeness that you are trying to recognize and understand through the rational logic of your mind, I can say only: give them up. They will do you no good. You will not find the answers there. You will not find the answers when you continue to recognize barriers and limitations within your thinking processes. Let go.

How did you let go?

The simplest way I can explain it was that I was able to let go at the time that it finally dawned upon me that there was nothing real to cling to, that it was only a thought process that I had made up.

Is there ever a time that the thought process that is creating this illusion does not exist?

The moment you decide it is not so.

What I'm asking may be obviously true for you but . . .

Nothing is true for me that is not true for you and I am not speaking in the framework of intellectual knowledge. This is something that you continue to grapple with thinking, "It's easy for you now that you're over there," but there is no difference between where I am and where you are except in what we believe is true.

Where does this thought then exist that what we are experiencing is this illusion?

It exists in each moment that you interpret free will to mean choice. To see choice, as you understand it, is to create a sense of duality;

it is the making of opposites and it is the beginning of the thought process that appears to take you away from where you really Are. It is the reversal of that process that will restore your recognition that you have never left.

This is not a profound or complex situation. It is far more simple than you will allow yourself to realize. You think you must look for a formula or a way to adjust your thought patterns so that you may put yourself back into the space of Being. Here is the simplicity: choose it wholly, choose it totally. Concurrently and coincidentally, recognize that you have never really made another choice.

Grasp fully that when I say "illusion", what I refer to is the fact that you do not see or recognize yourself as being totally Awake. That is the illusion. And once you have made that choice, all other choices appear to have opposites . . . they take on many different shapes and forms, and they are as broad as you allow your mind to play with them.

It is difficult for you while in the illusion to own up to the fact that you chose to be here . . . and you can simply choose to leave. It is a thought process and only a thought process. That is why I continuously say, there is no "place" for you to go. There is nothing for you to do. Change your mind. I cannot give you a formula for doing this. That would be for me to reinforce that in reality you have done something, but in reality you have not. How can I give you a formula to undo something that you haven't done?

Be constant in your recognition that you are whole. You may not be consciously willing to accept the full meaning of that wholeness, but since wholeness is what you Are, you obviously know what it is. So whether or not you consciously accept it, affirm in your mind that you are it. Know that you are whole and that everything that you do, or perceive you do, is simply a tactic of your mind which you have chosen to experience to reinforce all of the other choices that you feel you have made. After all, if you felt that there had been no validity to those other choices, to those experiences that you have had, my goodness, what would that do to your ego?

Why did I choose to experience the ego and separation?

To have a meaningful understanding of the answer to this question, it is first necessary to firmly assure yourself that you did not specifically choose to experience separation and the consequence of all its accompanying beliefs. The Spirit that is the truth of your Being exists forever in a state of unity and complete harmony with the whole of Creation. *This cannot and will not ever change.* Within this state of Being you would refer to as bliss, there is no awareness that there could be an experience contrary to this.

You did not consciously choose what has resulted in your current perception of separation for the idea itself had no meaning to you. There was no scheme to "play" at separation for awhile, slipping in and out of your wholeness at will. There was but a moment you could think of as there being a wondering if there was something more or beyond your awareness. In that instant, infinite fantasies of differences came and passed away. And in that instant existed all of what you now perceive as time and space.

You but seemed to make a choice that seemed to make a world which could exist apart from what is Creation. Why you thought you chose something in the past is irrelevant. Realize that in this present moment you can choose to know the truth, and that decision cannot be denied you.

A Concept of Simplicity

What can we choose to do that would best aid in the Awakening process?

There is only one choice for you to consciously make and that is the choice to recognize your Being, to "wake up" to your whole Mind. You might think that you have two things to do while you seem to be in a state of dreaming to enable you to come into the full realization of who you are: to allow yourself to step beyond the boundary of limitation your ego presents and then, subsequently, to express this Being that you Are, this Christ that is you. However, I will tell you in my terms there is only one thing to do because the second, through the experience of the first, will simply occur.

Once the recognition of who you are again becomes the reality in your conscious Mind, you will discover the natural thing to do is simply to be it. This requires no effort. It requires no doing. It is an activity of just reflecting who you Are. The process that you go through in trying to make this happen becomes an ego event. The ego can present to you the theory that this entire process becomes one of needing to conform to the other basic ego patterns which entail striving, feeling the need to "do." This translates into the ego continuing to be in charge, directing your thinking through the various events and experiences that you choose. It will suggest that you need to judge and interpret them, to react to them in such a way that it will be a positive experience and, therefore, helpful in this waking up process.

As I have said many times before, you are Awake. You think you are dreaming, and that is the illusion. If you can grasp the idea that the reality of you already Is, and already is expressing, then it will be significantly easier for you not to feel an ego need to direct this activity.

This is not new information. What I'm attempting to have you understand is that to play the ego's game is sometimes the easiest way to get you started out of the paths and patterns established by the ego. I am also stating that you are now ready to look at the synopsis, or short cut. You are ready for this because you have come to a point where you have found the various tactics you have tried to aid you in your enlightenment seem to be getting fuzzy; they seem to be misdirecting you and keeping you in a state of confusion. This is absolutely necessary for the ego to preserve its sense of limitation upon you. Let me restate that there is only one thing to remember and that is you are already Awake . . . you simply refuse to believe it. And it is in this refusal that you remain in the domain of limitation.

You will never see or experience any more or less than what you accept in your conscious mind as being true.

If you concentrate on the awareness that you are already fully Awake and there is nothing you can do to change that reality, that what you are trying to come to is the recognition, the remembering of that reality, then you will approach choices and circumstances in quite a different light.

A Dialogue on Awakening

How do I know when I'm getting direction from my higher Self?

It is the feeling of relaxing into something, the lack of the need to have a determination to overcome anything, that ultimately brings you into the recognition of that which you are seeking. The reason for this is very simple. When you determine to do something, you lower yourself to the ego level of thinking and you erect a barrier to the flow of information that comes to you from your whole Self, the Self that goes beyond the limitation of your ego mind.

I fear that I won't get direction from my whole Self. I guess the reason that I say that is because so often when I have asked for direction, to my knowledge I haven't received it.

You are expecting to hear the angel's trumpets, but this is not the way you communicate with your Self or with me. You listen to the voice that brings you peace. However mundane and familiar or unfamiliar that voice sounds, you can rest assured that you are hearing the voice of your Self when you hear it with a sense of peace. When you are in conflict, which you most certainly are when you are striving, you will not experience peace and you will know that you are experiencing the voice of the ego.

You are seeking something which you have imagined in your mind to be far more complex than it actually is. The quiet voice that brings you peace is the one that you have heard many times and not given credibility to.

It's interesting that when I ask that voice for teaching, I get beautiful answers but when I ask for guidance I don't get answers. I feel then that I get thrown back on my own resources and that puts me back into effort.

What you have been seeking for is advice on what to do and the fact of the matter is, it makes little difference what you do. The difference is why you do it, and how you do it . . . not on what you are doing.

I think death would bring me peace. I would like to get out of this.

What you are saying, is that you would like to find a way to escape and I will tell you now, there is no escape in death. Death is merely a door which goes from one room to the next. What you find in that room as you pass through the door is what you carry with you as you make the passage. And if it is escape you seek through death, then you will shortly find an equal desire to escape from that room back to the room of physical life.

Well, if death isn't the escape, what is the escape?

Why do you seek for escape?

Because I'm unhappy.

Where lies your freedom to happiness?

I thought that once I knew who I am, I would be free and happy.

That is undeniably true. What I am telling you is that what you picture as the world of death and what you now conceive of as the world of physical life is no different. What you perceive as the world of life versus the world of death bears no relevance on your waking up. The waking up process takes place in your mind, and that mind is with you in either event. Strange as it may seem to you at this moment, the options and choices that you have available to you in this realm make it far easier for you to choose to be Awake.

Yet, I have chosen to be Awake years and years ago and I'm not Awake yet!

You are looking for a magic formula. You are looking for a yardstick or a criterion that will either tell you that you are this far along toward being Awake, or that you have not made sufficient progress. You will find that this is not how it works.

How does it work?

The first thing for you to recognize is that you are already Awake. You are pretending not to be. The dream experience that you perceive yourself as being in is your pretending not to be Awake.

Begin by accepting completely that you are the perfected thought of God. You may intellectually say that you understand this, but you do not believe it. How could you possibly say that you did believe it and then in the next breath say, "I am struggling to be Awake." It is a matter of acceptance of what already is and that requires no struggle. It does require a sense of surrender with the sure knowledge that you are surrendering to your Self, to the wholeness of the Christ.

Why don't I trust myself? When I say my "Self," am I really meaning God?

You do not trust your Self because you have taught yourself to rely on the judgment of others as being the standard of your worth. You have perceived that evaluation to prove you to be insufficient, thereby judging yourself to be rejected. This ultimately leads you to the conclusion that you are not trustworthy. These are all things that appear to you to be outside your Self.

I am amazed at the amount of anger that I seem to have towards God. It's God's fault that I'm here. He puts a person in a hellhole and then does nothing to help us!

I will tell you that this feeling is true for everyone who does not perceive himself to be Awake. The degree to which you feel it and feel yourself expressing it is new to you and surprising because you have never expressed it in that fashion before. It is not an emotion or feeling which surfaced suddenly, but one that you have carried with you for far longer than it would be beneficial to remind you.

I would like to get rid of that feeling.

Then allow me to help you in this way. God does not see you as being separate from His Mind. God does not hear you in any utterance that is reflective of your thought of being separate from His Mind. God sees you only as you are and that is in a state of perfection.

Then why doesn't He reveal that to me so that I can see it too?

For God to acknowledge in any way that you were dreaming would be His support of your illusion and this is not possible.

Can He let me see me as He sees me? That wouldn't be supporting an illusion.

You are suggesting that your choice not to acknowledge your Self be revoked by God. I am saying to you that He does not acknowledge that choice as being real. He does not see you as ever having left your place in His Mind. He sees you as perfect. It is only your unwillingness to accept His vision that keeps you entombed within your limited vision. I will tell you now: I am acknowledging to you, as the Son of God, that I see with His eyes, and I see your perfection. Now, I have given you the acknowledgment that you have requested. How does that change your thinking? When you heard my words, did you release yourself? Did you feel the bonds fall away.

No. I felt very hopeless and helpless.

So you see, it is truly not God's acknowledgment that you seek, but your own.

So how can I come into that acknowledgment? Just to say the words, "I am whole, I am complete, I am pure," that doesn't do it for me.

Of course, it will not do it for you. It requires surrendering to the feeling that I have mentioned. It is a surrender to truth. And I cannot make it more complex. I cannot tell you how to surrender to the reality of who you are.

Why can't you tell me? That's what I need to hear!

When I have said to you, "Surrender," you heard me not. The frustration that you feel is because you expect someone to do it for you and this can never be. It is impossible for you to be a victim in any way, and could I reach to you now and by the simple act of laying my hand on your shoulder, clear your vision of the clouds which have kept you from seeing your own divinity, I would have made you a victim. Because there would have been a force outside of yourself that could have brought anything to you. And this would also mean that God created you a captive and not a free soul.

I don't think then that I understand what surrender means. I've so often said to God, "I give you my heart, my feeling, my soul, my will," but I'm not aware that anything has happened. It's as if He hasn't said, "Okay, thanks, Kid. I accept your surrender. I'll take over now."

Exercising the Will of God can only be recognized by you as being the Will of God when you know it as your own expression of peace and harmony. There is nothing for God to take over as you surrender to His Will.

He has to let me know what His Will is for me to surrender to it, doesn't He?

God's Will now, as it always has been, is for you to experience only that which Is, for you to experience and be only Love with the sure knowledge that you are seeing yourself as an extension of His perfection. And there is nothing for you to do to accomplish this because it is your natural state of Being.

I don't see why I don't know what my natural state of Being is.

Allow me to say this to you. You are totally absorbed in looking for a confirmation of your dream as being real. You are expecting to see a reflection of the natural Self within this quiltwork of illusion. You will not find it here. And now the thought springs into your mind,

"But I just asked you about dying a few moments ago." When I say you will not experience it here, I mean you will not experience it within the framework of the thinking which you are currently utilizing.

I don't think anything on this earth can give me peace. This is why I have sought the spiritual awakening so desperately.

And where would you find your spiritual awakening?

Well, I thought a revelation of who I am would help. People have beautiful visions. . .

God gives you only what you Are. You choose everything that comes into your experience that is in conflict with this.

Why do I choose it?

More to the point, why do you choose now not to experience your connection, your joining, your real alignment with your natural Self? Why do you not remember or have the recognition that you have never been separate from the Mind of God? Why do you not hear me when I tell you that you have never left the Mind of God?

I hear you and I appreciate this time you have given me, but I am lost. I've lost myself and I don't know how to come back.

You feel yourself to be lost because you feel that for such a long period of time you have asked and not received and, therefore, you feel that there must be something else to ask for. The answers have not become more complex, only your sense of direction which is imposing the questions. The answers to your questions have always been the same. But because they have not resonated with you in a form that has been recognizable, you have continued to ask different questions.

I will make this suggestion to you. As opposed to feeling the frustration about not knowing how to wake up, accept my truth when I tell you that you are already Awake.

Now, for you to bring yourself to a point of recognition of the truth of which I speak, vow to yourself that you will do nothing that does not bring you peace. This will be a process that will be extremely difficult for you to begin, because what I am suggesting to you is the step that you have refused to take these many years. Yet, that is the one which will bring you into the ultimate recognition of who you really Are. In your vow to do nothing that does not bring you peace, you will be forced to very closely scrutinize the choices you have made which have not brought you peace. And it will be in this scrutiny that you will come to understand why you have developed such a sense of low esteem for yourself. You will discover all of the rationalizations that you have used in the past, and they will be a great temptation to continue. But you will, in fact, be separating the wheat from the chaff in your mind, and it will be this process that ultimately brings you the clarity of the loving choices which will put you in touch with your Self.

You desperately seek for one to join with, for one outside yourself to give you love. But I must tell you this joining is impossible without loving yourself. I am not saying that you could not at this moment experience, by comparison, a very loving relationship. What I am telling you is that no relationship in its final outcome can meet your expectations of love and joining until you have accepted yourself as being worth loving. It is not possible for you to give or to receive anything that you have not acknowledged and accepted within yourself.

In this pursuit of peace, I can see running into some snags. For instance, I can see that I get some peace in knowing that I am earning some money by teaching pupils, but I don't have a lot of peace teaching, I'd rather not teach. So there is peace and there is not peace, all at the same time. Which way would I go?

Once you have made a commitment to do only those things that bring you peace, you will find peace in whatever you do. You see, the lack of peace has nothing to do with the activity. It has only to do with the confusion in your mind about the many things that are taking place in your life.

Is God living His life through me?

It would not be appropriate for me to say that God does not recognize illusion and then to tell you that God lives His life through your illusion.

On the other hand, I will say to you when you are Realized, when you are recognizable to your Self as being only the extension of the Mind of God, you will clearly realize that you are the only way for God to be expressed.

In this world.

In the world of Reality. You are still confused when I talk about the world of Reality. You conjure up different times, different places, different worlds. The world of God is within your mind. It is within the clarity that recognizes the Reality of God. That is your whole Mind which is not deluded by illusion. There is a great deal of difficulty in accepting a definition of illusion to something which you perceive as being so real.

I will say to you again, there is only one thing that is really going on. That is the expression of the Mind of God, and that expression is recognizable as being only peaceful, only harmonious and in a constant state of unconditional love. And when, in your mind, you experience any thought that is not reflective of these traits, then you are experiencing an illusion of truth. That is why my suggestion to you was to vow to choose only those things that brought you peace. Because it will be through the practice of this that you will more closely align your thinking to reality. And it will be that process that will change your patterns of thinking to become more closely aligned with your natural thought processes which are truly reflective of the Mind of God. It will be through the establishing of this parallel process that you will make the transition and take the final step to join with your natural Self, and in that joining, recognize the truth that you never left.

Is this going to take a long time?

The length of time involved in any undertaking is relative to your belief in the concept of time. And that is not an evasion of your question because you will find that when you are in a state of experiencing a more constant flow of peace in your life, the concept of time will become far less meaningful to you. Time is only experienced as a deterrent when you cling to the belief that what you are experiencing in the way of pain is something to be escaped from. The experience of joy and peace is one that is reflective of infinity because it carries no sense of fear. It is only the sense of fear that gives meaning to time.

Your reason, incidentally, for asking the question had little to do with wondering when you would be free, but a great deal to do with your wanting to establish another yardstick, a place at which you could arrive and then be able to make the judgment as to how effective this proposal I have given you has been in your life.

I thought the reason I asked was because I am feeling so discouraged. I've striven, I've worked so hard and so long that I am almost overwhelmed by the thought of more struggling .

But you see, what I have suggested to you is the elimination of more struggle.

Let me suggest a way for you to establish the validity of what I have said when I spoke to you about it being impossible for you to be a victim. Beyond your recognition at this moment, you already do have a clear realization of the sensation of peace. Trust this to be true and it will come into focus. In your heart of hearts, you already recognize most clearly you do have the power and the recognition to call peace into your experience. Call upon it and trust it to be so. You are not a victim. I would not suggest anything to you that was beyond your grasp.

I have the confidence in your ability to choose peace. If you need to rely upon my confidence, then do so. But recognize that it is only my confidence that you are relying upon. It is not my choice that will be forced upon you, but only my confidence in your choice. Choose peace, and allow it to be so. I said to you before that this would be the path that would be most difficult for you to take because it is the one you have refused to embark upon before.

I will pursue it. I will work upon it.

No work, please. Trust that if you choose it so, it is done. And to see the results of what you have chosen, you have but to relax and trust and experience.

Were it possible for you to experience my physical countenance, I would be smiling. And I would be smiling because I cannot see any side to you that is not reflective of perfection.

You mentioned before though, that you were aware that I was very frustrated.

I am aware of your feelings for yourself and I am aware of my feelings for you. And while the two in reality are one, your perception is one which does not reflect truth. I see your distortion, but it does not blind me to the truth. I may look through your eyes into your dream, but I recognize your dream as being unreal. That is why we truly are joined. I have shared your experience of both truth and illusion.

Balance

Would you speak to us of balance? Of how to live on this earth in a body and also to be aware of the Reality of who we really are as an extension of God?

Attempting to achieve a sense of balance between the infinite and the finite intellectually is much like juggling a combination of feathers and bowling balls. Pursuing the delicate feather as it floats free of the world's gravity awakens a hidden sensation of great joy. Then your ego screams in your ear that a ball the size of a bowling ball is about to drop on your head because you're chasing feathers instead of dealing with the "real world." You therefore see the two as incompatible because you are trying to make them merge. Your intellect will not accept the notion of a bowling ball being supported by a feather. The infinite and the finite are not compatible. One exists and it is truth. The other does not and is but an illusion of truth.

Be clear that what you are attempting to balance is truth and illusion. It becomes an effort to compromise with truth until you feel safe enough to let go of illusion. You will find this balancing act ultimately becomes an exercise in futility, producing extreme frustration. The feather will not even support a ping-pong ball. The solution then, does not become one of finding a balance or compromise while you're in the process of trying to decide when to let go of your misperception. It becomes one of removing your focus from the misperception. You will pass through illusion to truth by focusing on truth, not by looking for ways to leave illusion behind or make it more comfortable on your journey through.

Please do not interpret this to be a suggestion that you project yourself to some point in the future when you have fully accepted the truth of your Self, or that you be anything less than completely joyful each and every moment. Living in truth is completely joyful!

My suggestion is not to focus on finding a balance between truth and illusion but to accept truth by choosing peace and joy in your life.

It is often thought that as the journey of Awakening progresses, there are other places where you will go to receive progressively greater wisdom to enhance your process of becoming enlightened. Various solar systems and planets have been described as the setting for this purpose. They hold out to you the promise of being magical places inhabited only by "Master Teachers" who will shape and mold your conscious awareness enabling you to also become a Master Teacher, a Divine Being.

The process sounds reasonable to you because it parallels your systematically progressive educational programs. It also relieves you of the responsibility for making your own choices, here and now, to remember that you are already a Master Teacher and as completely Divine as you ever will be. No one will teach you to awaken to this at some future time because there is only one time, now, and only one place, here, where you are now. Future awakening is not possible, for the future will always remain somewhere ahead of you. It cannot come closer and you will never be in it because it is only a concept of separation.

I would like to suggest that you try something. Allow yourself to envision the Mind of God. Be open to the feeling that comes. You are more aware of this than you consciously know. Within the scope of this Vision will be, as fully as you are able to allow it, all that exists; the totality of all Creation in its infinite expression. There will be no edges. There will be no definition or description of places within it. It will exist in wholeness.

And now I say that this is where you reside. This is the scope of your playground. Where you play within it is only determined by the limitation that you place upon your mind being able to experience it. As your conscious mind expands and each barrier is removed, the depth of your experience of the Mind of God opens to you. It has been described as levels of consciousness and ascending planes, but this is not appropriate. This is whole territory with no fences or boundaries or edges or distinctions. It exists wholly as the full expression of Creation which is God. And you are in the picture wholly. It is only through your putting a frame that has finite, limited edges around your own experience that you limit your experience of the whole. That is why I say there is no place to go. There is no place where you are not.

I find myself continually oscillating back and forth between my lower self and who I am. Is there any process to remind me of who I am?

That is the process, to continue to remind yourself of who you are. You see, once you really come down to that core issue of "Am I really acceptable?" It leads you to the exploration of "Who am I?" If I need to know whether or not I am acceptable then I must identify myself. I need to know if who I am has any worth. I suggest to you that if who you are has no worth, there is no worth in the Mind of God.

This is an issue that you each must face. Ask first, "Am I an expression, an extension of the Mind of God?" And if you answer, "Indeed I am," and then refuse to accept the value of who you Are, you have refused to accept the value of the Mind of God.

You see, this is the key to your really being able to admit that you have only perceived yourself as separate from the Mind of God. If you can overcome that hurdle, then the answer to your question will be obvious, will it not? If you are an undiluted, undistorted expression of the Mind of God, and if you have no value, there is no value in the Mind of God. Ask the question. You know the answer.

That's really what we come to each time that we disavow the love that exists within us as being the only true expression there is of us. It is no more complex than I am telling you this very instant. If there is value in the Mind of God, if there is love in the Mind of God and you are an expression of it, why don't you accept it?

Do you want a definition of being Awake versus being asleep? You've just got it. It is only that; it is your acceptance of the recognition of who you Are. And there is obviously nothing to do to attain that except believe it. So whatever process you may ask for or concoct for yourself, it is a process with but this one goal: making you believe what you already know to be true.

Now that I have sounded so grim, let me give you the bright side. There is no way for you not to do this. It is who you Are, and you may not hide from it forever. Your memory does not become lost because you do not appear to use it. And in the moment of recognition, you will remember instantly that it has never been gone. It is the same experience that you have now as you awaken from a dream when you are sleeping.

I have received the guidance to act or pretend as if I were Awake. Would you care to comment on this?

This process that you are engaged in is wonderful. It is precisely that which will create a new thought pattern. It is consciously recognizing that you are Awake. That process will open you to an easier way of remembering. I congratulate you upon it.

I would like to refer to what many focus on as the goal of waking up. The practice of acting and believing that you are Awake, approaching each situation that you encounter by extending the Love that you are, is contradictory to the goal of being Awake. By your establishing in your mind that there is a goal, you are saying that there is something to work towards. The practice that you are engaged in is a practice of saying, "I am already it." This being so, what is there to work toward? You are already there. Stick with the plan of acting Awake. It is the essence of what I have tried to convey.

It is this type of practice that changes the mind pattern and which will lift you from experiencing or perceiving situations in an illusory fashion. And each time that you eliminate a particular situation in which you are seeing illusion, you permit yourself to sneak a little closer to confirming the feeling of being Awake.

I feel wonderful when I do this, but I am uncomfortable saying this to others.

Then keep the process to yourself until you become more comfortable with it, and you will. Just act in a fashion that illustrates that you are Awake. No one will be uncomfortable with that!

How can emotions be best utilized in the Awakening process?

By first recognizing they have been a solid anchor into the world of illusion. There is but one feeling you have that is currently categorized as emotion, but is truly not, and that is the feeling of Love. Love, as you will come to understand, is most inappropriately categorized as emotion. To specifically answer your question, let us say succinctly: Understand that emotions serve well the ego, but do not serve the spirit. Emotions are derived as expressions from ego activities.

There is that which the ego would present to you that says, " If I must give up my emotions there will be nothing left of me to experience or feel. Therefore, why should I wake up?" Understand clearly that what I am attempting to define for you is the difference between recognizing those feelings that you perceive to be produced by your ego, and those feelings produced as a reflection of your state of Being. I will tell you there is much more fullness, a sense of completeness, which exists in the expression of your Self that cannot be reflected to you through the experience of the ego perception.

Please keep in mind what we have said before. The ego is merely a limited sense of your Self. It is the sense of yourself that prevents you from seeing the wholeness of your Self. Therefore, even to the logical mind, does it not follow that anything you could experience in a sense of limitation would be more fully, more completely, more joyously felt and experienced without a sense of limitation?

The greatest aid in understanding your emotions as they pertain to your awakening is to let them go as they are an additional sense of limitation. Do not struggle to become a person who does not show emotion, but allow yourself to be recognized as a person who expresses a greater sense of himself. And the joy that will be reflected will be recognizable to you and to others as being a reflection of your Being, a picture of your Self in a state of peace. And do not worry about the definition of what is an emotion and what is more accurately known or defined as an extension of your Being.

It seems quite clear that there are emotions that are a hindrance to one's Awakening, yet I would like to know where compassion fits in here. Does it need to be released to Awaken?

Let me say first that I am attempting to define what is the state of Reality as opposed to supporting an illusion of reality. In Reality you may be certain there exists nothing to which there is an opposite. Therefore, I attempt to direct your attention away from concepts that have meanings of positive and negative or good and bad, because these concepts are reflective only of a state of illusion to truth.

The feeling of compassion is the one which probably is most misunderstood and feared by those who are attempting to identify themselves as a Being of Love. The reason the difficulty arises is simply this: you see yourself and identify your Being as a body, but it is not. You do not accept the fact that you are at this moment, a totally undistorted expression of the Mind of God. And because you do not, you see a need to have pity upon yourself and others who see likewise. I am sure that it would shock you significantly were I to tell you there is no compassion in the Mind of God. What exists there is only the expression of truth. God's Vision, being real, sees you only in your state of Reality. It sees you only in the perfection in which you truly exist. And to this, ascribe joy and not compassion.

When you come to the understanding that the truest expression of yourself as an extension of the Mind of God is only to reflect the love that lies therein, you will see there is no need for compassion; there is nothing to be compassionate about. So am I then telling you that while you dwell in a state of dream to go about expressing cruelty? Obviously not. What I am encouraging you to do is to go about expressing your Self as an extension of the only thing that truly exists and that is a state of perfect love! Because it is in the doing of this that you will recognize it. It is by what you teach that you have decided what it is you have chosen to learn. Does this sound familiar? Teach only love. That truly is all you are.

If, while you are seeing yourself as going through the process of waking up, the expression of an emotion which you view as compassion is helpful to you in understanding yourself as being only love, then express compassion. I have told you why compassion does not exist in the Mind of God, but I do not encourage you at any time to go beyond what you are willing to accept at this moment as being an accurate expression of your awakening process. If the expression of compassion fits into that process, then use it as you would any other tool. But were I not to have given you the complete picture, so to speak, it would not have resonated with you as being truth and this is what you have asked to be reminded of.

Let's say it one more way: express love in any way that best suits you and your definition of it at the moment it is being expressed, and recognize thoroughly that this is what is happening—that you are expressing love in the most complete way you have chosen to understand it in the moment and feel wonderful about doing it! Do not approach it or express it from the standpoint of saying, "Well, I'm expressing love in the only way I understand it at the moment, and it's probably not the best, but I'll go ahead and do it anyway." Express it knowing that you are being it.

When we are not in the physical dimension, are we aware that we are perfection?

The essence of the question is whether or not your awareness changes automatically as you experience yourself without a body. The nature of your experiences will change, because you currently define them in terms of how they will affect your body. But the meaning of your experiences, then as now, is determined by your perception of what constitutes the true nature of your Being. Having or not having a body does not automatically change your mind about who you are. The acceptance of your perfection is as readily available to you now as it ever will be. This statement would be equally true if you did not experience yourself as having a body.

Does the ego exist in that other dimension?

Your ego is not a part of the physical body. Your ego is a limitation within your Mind. Your ego exists as an expression of limitation. Any dimension where you happen to be, you are there with your Mind. And the limitation of your Mind will exist until you have chosen not to experience it any longer.

An Hourglass of Divine Consciousness

What is it that I need to do to access my higher Self?

There is a place of trust that at this moment you are not consciously familiar with. It is a place where you feel the footing is very soft and tenuous. You have built a pattern of feeling needy—needy of confirmations, needy of loving yourself. If you could envision yourself as being two different people, you would see one of them standing with arms spread wide, beckoning you to come nearer, wishing that you would let go of the reluctance to embrace. You would see then the other aspect of yourself standing back and looking in awe at the one who was beckoning and feeling totally disconnected.

You do see your Self, that Self that possesses the wisdom that you seek at this moment, but you are not in a position of allowing yourself to be in absolute acceptance of it. You do hear, but you hear in a way that is intellectually pleasing and yet emotionally unacceptable to the conscious self that you now see yourself as being. What I am telling you is that you are already there, but you are unaccepting of finding yourself being there. It is this lack of acceptance which filters out the truth of what you are hearing.

There is much you have understood as having application in your life from what you have considered to be a spiritual point of view, but you have dissociated this spiritual point of view from that which you call your practical life. In other words, you feel that it's fine to ingest the spiritual knowledge, but you find it difficult to see its practical applicability to solving your daily problems. I encourage you to understand that there is no distinction between what you are understanding as spiritual input and practical input. If you could look at it all as being your input and allow it to be integrated in a practical fashion, you would become more accepting of it as you saw it begin to work.

What I am speaking of is not something that I would refer to as grandiose or complex, but more simply as the application of letting go of your fear and opening up a space which is big enough to allow more of your loving, peaceful Self to come in. I am not speaking in terms that are metaphorical. I am suggesting that all that happens to you is first taking place in your mind. Your mind is now perceived as being full of the thoughts that you currently have, and there is no space for your thoughts to take on a different attitude.

One of the most practical applications of learning to stay in the moment is simply this: a mind that is full of fears and apprehensions that have been made and confirmed by past thinking patterns sees no space for alternative thinking. It is a mind that sees itself as being full. It has misidentified the reason the problems seem to be present, seeing them as having originated from an outside source, and demands that all your attention be focused on formulating plans which will solve the problems. While you are engaged in this process, your mind is closed to anything else. It is filled with the problems and seeking ways to solve them. When fear is present, your attention will focus on anticipating circumstances or events similar to those which have manifested this fear to you in the past, thus appearing to confirm their reality. Because your attention is on them, you will again make the experience of them, deepening your belief in their validity. And so the cycle becomes imprinted in your mind as a pattern which self-perpetuates.

A mind that knows only this instant does not recognize the past and is not concerned or fearful of the future. And that does create space, an openness into which this dialogue, this wisdom that you are seeking, may penetrate. It will be into that space, as you allow yourself to be in that frame of mind, that the wisdom will come and you will recognize very clearly where it is coming from.

So when you ask how you can be in contact with your Self, I am saying you already are, but because your mind is so full you do not recognize its Presence. So every now and again, empty out the cup by being present only in this instant.

Could you share what the process of emptying out the cup would be like?

Breaking old patterns and replacing them with new patterns is difficult enough to do, and breaking old patterns and allowing no new patterns to take their place will be even more difficult for you to do. I will suggest a process and a procedure if you would care to try. I am in no way attempting to discourage you by telling you that you will not find this easy, although the process is quite simple. I am telling you this so that you will not become discouraged if at first you do not find that you are easily able to do it.

An Image Given:

Envision an hour glass with sand in the upper half, floating in a clear, cool pond which is nestled in a beautiful meadow lush with wild flowers. The rim of the glass and sand is just level with the surface of the pond. The hourglass is a metaphor of your mind, completely filled as the sand symbolically illustrates. It is so full that the water of the pool, representing the Christ consciousness, the stream of your fully conscious Self, can only ripple across the top.

As you watch the sand slowly drain away, allow your mind to open up space as you see the sand slowly going down and more space being created until the sand is all gone. As the sand has been draining away, the water from the pool of consciousness just naturally fills the space. Its flow has a very gentle, peaceful and loving feeling. It is this feeling that reassures you that simply because the sand thoughts have drained out doesn't mean there is nothing left except a void. But more appropriately, the space is filled with this flow of feeling that is totally cohesive and not fragmented and into which you can just allow yourself to become safely immersed. As you have this Vision and see yourself becoming totally immersed in it, you know that what is happening is that you are allowing your divine Mind to embrace you.

Allow the feeling that being in this fluid is like being in the womb of your Divine Mind. This feeling, if you hold it and allow it to give you a sense of nurturing, will encourage you to see yourself as being born into the divinity of your natural Self. While you are engaged in this process, you won't be receiving answers to any specific questions, or trying to solve any pressing problems. The very act of your experiencing yourself being in this womb of Divinity will begin to open you consciously to all of the feelings that will allow you to recognize those problems that you have been working on for what they really are, and to keep them in a perspective that will no longer make them seem fearful to you.

Hold no expectations. Allow the process itself to unfold for you and allow yourself to be open to the experience of that unfoldment. It will be that which will keep you constant and will keep your attention clearly focused on right now.

This would be in a meditative state?

Yes. The most peaceful state that you are able to allow yourself to be in. The more frequently you attempt this, the more completely you will find you are able to allow yourself to become immersed in it. As you envision this fluid, see yourself dissolve into it, and know that what is happening is that you are opening yourself to merge with your Divine Mind. Enter into this process in total trust, absolutely total trust, that what your divine Mind represents for you will be made known to you in ways that require no questioning. It will become a process of Knowing.

Thank you. How can I serve you?

There is but one service and that is the service to your Self, your capital "S" Self. As I say this to you, understand quite clearly that this is in no way an ego-involved statement. The service to your Self is a service to the Christ, and it will be through your performing whatever act most clearly represents this service to you that brings you into clearer focus of your being the Christ. It will be through the unfoldment and Vision of yourself as the Christ that you will see most truly the service of extending the act of becoming, unfolding and exposing itself as being what it is. The expression of what it is, of what you Are, is the loving Mind of God.

For the Mind of God to be recognized, it must be experienced. It will be through the fulfillment of your experience of It and your natural extension of that experience which will fulfill your purpose. It is the continuing fulfillment of that purpose that is the extension of the Mind of God which is known as Creation. All that exists within Reality exists within you and is expressed as being the uncompromising Love of the Father.

So now we come full circle. Why is it necessary to wake up to recognize your Self? Because that is the only way you can experience the Love of God. It will be through your experience of it that you will continue to extend it, and it is through your extension of it that others will see themselves reflected in its light. In that Light, all of Creation will be recognized. And I will say to you that this Light is always on, this Light is always being seen, but it is not always being recognized. So I encourage you to think of this act of waking up as being one of pushing aside the veil to see what is already there. This will make it seem far less complex, that there is far less to "do" than you might otherwise think.

There is always that aspect, that human trait which says, "I have heard this before," and continues to drive you towards new ways of seeking to wake up. I ask you to understand that this is the single process that keeps the ego image of you alive.

What you have just described sounds like a very direct route.

The route is quite direct. How could it be less than direct when you hold the recognition that you are already It? There is nothing for you to become, there is only for you to recognize that you already Are. And that realization is most easily come by as you allow yourself, in your current frame of mind, to become most similarly like that which you are when you are in recognition of your divine Mind; that is, to be in a state that trusts and refuses to acknowledge fear; that accepts only that which brings you peace and sees Love beyond the facade of hate.

Why is it so easy and simple for me to hear this now, to feel and to connect up, but not at other times? What do I have to eliminate?

First eliminate the thought that there is something to eliminate. What we are dealing with is a pattern of thinking. And what we are trying to accept is the notion that there need be *no* pattern of thinking. Patterns of thinking are developed to avoid having to trust your Self in the moment. That is why I suggested the process of allowing yourself to be nurtured by your Divine Mind so that it will become naturally more easy for you to trust that Mind, and not to feel that you have to rely on the limited mind as your pattern has been to do this for many, many years.

Resisting Awareness

Is my resistance to accessing greater awareness a resistance to trusting my whole Self?

I can tell you that your resistance has a lot to do right now with your feeling that you would somehow lose contact with those around you, with those who do not seem to be seeking their spiritual identity. And were you to let go, to just allow yourself to remember, you fear you would somehow find yourself disconnected from them.

Is that true? Are those fears true?

No. Just the opposite is true. You now see and experience everyone through your perception of what is real. As you expand your state of awareness, you will merely experience more of the truth of everyone. Similarly, do you recall as a small child thinking that your parents were gods, that they knew everything? And then, as you began to grow older and more wise in the ways of the world, you began to realize that your parents didn't know anything, that you knew it all? And then one day, suddenly, you turned around and said, "Good grief! How could my parents get so smart so fast?" It's that transition. It's because you suddenly allowed yourself into the awareness of the wisdom they already possessed that you could then look upon them and see that they had it. Now that's a parallel; its not exactly what happens, but it is similar.

You see, everybody at this very moment is Awake. All of us are as God created us in a state of perpetual perfection. When we don't see that, then we see through the lens that *A Course in Miracles* refers to as illusion; you see an illusion of the truth, a shadow of the truth. As you allow your mind to expand and encompass a greater degree of truth, then you will see that greater degree of truth reflected in everything and everyone around you.

You now only experience that which will fit into your script. And your composing of that script is encompassed within the limitations of your perceptions at any given moment. The world around you is as real and Awake as you are capable of seeing it, because you have shaped your experience within the limits of your perception. If the limits of your world existed beyond your belief in them, then it would always be possible for something or someone to make a victim of you, or for someone to drag you down or hold you back. That's a very difficult thing to grasp because you look at the world around you and say, "That's just the way the world is." The only way to change that is for you to come to the understanding, the absolute knowing, that enables you to look at the world around you and say, "This is the world that exists as I see it, and because I see it that way, it exists that way. As I change the way I look at the world, the world seems to change." But, you see, the world never changes—there is no world to change! There is only our self-perception which changes and then things around us must follow suit.

If you mistakenly believe that the world changes and therefore, you allow yourself to change, you are confusing cause and effect. The world is always the effect; the cause is how you think, where you are in your mind. As the cause changes, there is nothing else for the effect to do except to reflect the cause.

So if I do not anticipate problems with those around me as I choose to Awaken, I will not have any.

That is absolutely right. You can only experience those things that you have chosen, the script that you have written in your mind.

A New Age?

Are we close to experiencing a new age of more awakened Beings on this plane? Are we evolving into a higher consciousness at this time?

I would encourage you here to remember that in a state of Reality, there is no definition of time. Time is a limitation. Limitations do not exist in the Mind of God. For me to try to confirm to you the importance of a definition of your dream would be inappropriate. The definition of a thousand or of a million years of "radiance" is one that is arrived at by the ego. The truth of you is infinite. Infinity takes place this moment and only now. When you adopt this concept, when you allow your mind to become free of any other concept except that you are, in Reality, a totally, fully realized expression of your Creator, you will recognize that your choosing to be aligned with that truth is available to you on a moment's notice. What I would refer to as the instant of Reality would be described as infinite.

Evolution by degrees is the perfect description of the supreme achievement of the ego. That keeps you in a constant state of allowing yourself to believe that there is a goal just around the corner as opposed to the recognition that if you are the perfect creation of the Father, what could there be to evolve into except the memory of It, and memory is instantaneous.

Is this, then, only an ego concept that we are entering a new age of awareness?

Again, I would ask you to define or to clarify for yourself the meaning of "age." If age connotes in your thinking a period of time, then you may rest assured that it is a concept that is derived from limitation, or what you would refer to as ego. I encourage you to allow your focus to be centered on the Mind of God. The Mind of God exists only now. This does not mean, nor should you translate that to be static or in any way lacking movement, because the Mind of God is in a constant state of movement and that movement is you, His Son. Your expression of the infinite aspects of God is the movement of Creation, of the universe, of the Mind of God, however you would wish to describe it. There is one cause and one effect. The Mind of God is the cause, and you, as His Created Son, are the effect. And it is the expression of the effect that constitutes the movement of the universe.

But in the flow of history I see this movement unfolding that seems dependent on time. How does one then reconcile this flow of collective development?

I would bring your attention to what I will describe as a fear of the unknown. What makes it appear to be more palatable for you is the feeling that you are in the company of others, that you are taking along baggage of the known in the form of what you would describe as other people. This gives you the comfort of walking into the unknown because you feel you are walking in together, and somehow there is a feeling of comfort in numbers.

The historical facts and accumulation of data as you are seeing them is the face the world has presented to you and which has kept you from seeing the truth. You will not find the truth of you evidenced anywhere in the world of illusion. It would be much like your attempting to learn geometry in a textbook of English literature; the answers are not to be found there.

Then the condition of Heaven on earth is not a condition of the earth or of its inhabitants as much as it is an individual experience.

Nothing for you is a condition that exists outside of yourself. Your residing in Heaven is totally dependent upon your state of mind and your choosing that state of mind to reflect whatever aspects of Heaven you have chosen them to be. Heaven exists within you eternally, as eternally as does your Divinity. It is only the recognition of your Divinity that allows you to see where you have always been. Heaven for you can be achieved on earth if you are on earth; Heaven for you would exist on Mars if you were on Mars. There is no place for you to be except at that point within your mind that you recognize yourself as either being an expression of the Christ or something other than that. And whatever you experience will only be a function of whichever state of mind you are in at the moment.

Is it only by my coming into my Awakening that Heaven will come to earth? How is that going to express itself out to the rest of those 6 billion people?

Let me say that what you are attempting to do is to give your ego-limited mind an endless number of possibilities to dissect and analyze. There is but one answer to the question that you are asking, and you will not find it by asking a thousand other peripheral questions.

You do not see yourself as being a direct expression of God, and in this lack of sight you will not see anything else around you in any way that reflects that which is God. As you take each of these circumstances and situations and attempt to analyze them to perfection, wonder how you can bring them to perfection, you are attempting to rearrange your misperception. That will have no effect on the fact that the origin of your misperception is firmly rooted in who you think you are as opposed to who you really Are. You continue to deal with the effects and avoid approaching the cause.

The cause of every misperception that you have is based upon your lack of knowledge of who you Are. Until that misperception has been corrected, every misperception that flows from that central point will be equally incorrect. You must see through the eyes of truth to see truth. You may not look through the eyes of misperception and see truth. Your only choice, in the final analysis, is to decide whether or not you want to give up misperception.

Please define "misperception".

Misperception occurs when you do not see through the eyes of God, when you see anything less than the perfection of His Creation.

As you allow your perception to more closely parallel that of truth, you will more clearly see the truth of your brothers. You will not look at them through the eyes of limitation; you will look at them through the eyes of wholeness. You will see their wholeness, and you will recognize that the Mind of the Christ is always in a state of perfect functioning and perfect awareness. Because you see yourself as being in a limited state of awareness, you are presuming that is how everyone around you also sees themselves. And while this is a concept that will be difficult for your intellect to grapple with, I will tell you that it is only through your eyes, and the clarity that you allow yourself to see through those eyes, that you will see the reality of the Christ in its wholeness, in its completeness, in its state of being absolutely Awake. And you will recognize many familiar faces. There will be no sense of loneliness.

You see those around you only through the lens of your own awareness. You perceive that this is how they are. If you were always to believe this, then you must always believe that most of the Mind of Christ is asleep and therefore not functioning, not expressing the Love of God, the Reality of Creation. This is not true.

I would suggest to you that you just concern yourself with your own Awakening. Have the realization, the joyful anticipation, of what awaits you as you finally open your eyes and see. It will not be a vacant playground!

Chapter Two

Choosing Peace

"The reason to choose peace is that it is not of the illusion. It is a reflection of Reality. Choices made that do not bring you peace validate the illusion and keep your attention on it."

How To Find Peace

Would you please help me understand why I don't seem to be aware of Spirit within me? Why do I keep it outside my awareness?

Your current self awareness is based upon the presumption that you are separate from the Spirit that created you like and as a part of Itself, and while you reject this truth, you withhold It from your experience. To accept the Spirit of God as part of yourself, you must accept it as the essence of everything you see. Let me reassure you, however, that denying the Presence of God within you does not, in any way, alter what has always been and always will be. You are inseparable from your Source.

Is it that what I'm seeing is coming back and . . .

Let me make it a little easier for you. There are two things that you are struggling with right now: The first and foremost is lack of clarity. The second is believing that there is something going on in your life that is beyond your control.

Let's talk about the clarity. There is confusion in your mind as to exactly what it is that you can do to rectify what appears to be a resolution of your spiritual growth and your day to day activities as you see those activities pulling you away from your calm and peaceful center.

So, let's talk about a very basic issue. You have heard many times and expressed in many different ways that you make your own reality. I have said that you will experience what you choose to see. Boiling this down, what it simply means is that whatever is in your mind you will think that you are experiencing. I say you will "think" you are experiencing because in the world of dreams it is precisely that—a dream. But it comes to you as real and, therefore, we will refer to it in terms of being real within the dream.

What is in your mind you will see as being manifest in the physical world, in the dream. And when there is lack of clarity in your mind, there is obviously nothing for there to be outside your mind except an equal lack of clarity. It is the limited sense of your mind that you are now employing which allows you only to see that which you are dreaming about. What else could there be for you to dream about except what you make up in your mind? Therefore, whatever is in your mind is what you will dream about.

You will find it very helpful if you recognize with total clarity the absolute Truth that I'm giving to you at this moment. Because it is this Truth that will allow you to see vividly, on a moment to moment basis, exactly whether or not your mind is clear or unclear as you go through your daily activities. When you see them being chaotic, you will immediately know that this condition is reflective of your mind.

What you are wondering is how do you change all this. If it is in your mind, how else could you possibly change it except by changing your mind? What we are dealing with then is the creation of new thought patterns. It is difficult for you to recognize the chaotic thought patterns that currently exist in your mind because they have been there for such a long time. And you have become comfortable with the feeling of them—they have become familiar to you. Therefore, you identify yourself as being that way; that this is your natural or normal state of mind. So when I suggest to you it is as simple as changing your mind, it appears to be a very complex matter. And indeed, it will remain complex as long as you are of the opinion that what you are experiencing in the form of chaos is what you would refer to as "normal".

What you are really trying to achieve is a sense of peace. What I would suggest is this: as you are going through any process, recognize that you are going through it to attain a state of peace. Be aware that each thing you do, no matter what it may be, you are doing it to achieve peace. Recognize this as you approach the most mundane of tasks. With each thing you do, consciously repeat in your mind, "I do this to attain peace. I do this because it brings me peace." Become comfortable with that thought. Allow that thought to be with you consciously, in the beginning particularly when you are in easy moments of peace, when you do not seem to be disturbed by outside influences which would make peace difficult to experience.

Choose peace while you are brushing your teeth, choose peace when you view a beautiful flower. Choose peace when you feel someone chewing on your rear end.

Obviously, what we are doing here is establishing that pattern in your mind so that as you find yourself in the circumstances and situations that create the chaos that currently exists there, you will say, "I do this to bring me peace." And you will consciously have the opportunity to choose again. And please, don't be misled; don't allow the old patterns to take control. Don't feel that you are forced in any way to continue doing something that does not respond to your request for peace by saying, "I have to do this, I don't have another choice, I must do this." *You must do nothing that does not bring you peace.*

Now, there very well may be occasions when you are unwilling to respond by changing what you are doing, or changing your attitude about what you are doing in such a way that you recognize peace as a result. What I will suggest to you now is that you do not judge yourself as being guilty or negligent in any way for continuing with the activity that you are consciously aware is not bringing you peace. This would destroy the entire process, because very soon you would recognize that you didn't want to feel guilty any more about not choosing peace. Therefore, you would abandon the process and no longer continue to repeat the phrase, "I do this for peace." I suggest that on those occasions you alter the phrase and say, "I know I'm doing this and I know it's not going to bring me peace, and for whatever reason, I'm going to do it anyway, and it's okay." And then watch how the results will change because, as you give yourself permission to continue the activity that will not bring you peace and you do so in a frame of mind that is non-judgmental, you'll find the peace was there after all.

You seem to be punishing yourself for wanting so desperately to be Awake and not feeling yourself capable of achieving it. Allow me to tell you, there is nothing that can prevent you from remembering who you Are. The only thing that would appear to delay the process is the one that you are engaged in now, which is that of appearing to punish yourself for not now being aware of it. You do that because you have not chosen wholly to give it up. You have not chosen completely to step beyond this comfort zone that you are currently dreaming about and return to your natural, normal state of memory. That's what this process seems to be about.

Remember that this experience that seems to be so real, that seems to hold so much excitement, that seems to keep you so alive, is a mere shadow of your true experience of your Self. It is why you appear to creep up on this business called "Awakening." It seems to allow you to push back or expand the comfort zone little by little by little so that what you are stepping into has a ring of familiarity. And that, too, is okay. The thing you do that appears to make it more painful is to judge yourself as being guilty for not being capable of taking the leap. What I am trying to make clear is this: the feeling that is creating that confusion in your mind is one that is there because you know at the deepest level of your Being who you Are. And that truth seeps through, just a little, into your conscious awareness of this dream. So, as you appear to creep up on Reality, there is still that little Voice of your true Self saying, "You don't need to do this."

In everything you do, choose peace. In everything you do that you recognize does not bring you peace and you want to do it anyway, feel okay about it.

With this in mind, how does one deal with a stressful situation involving others in a dispute?

I would call your attention to the method of communication. When you are communicating with anyone, two things are apparently happening: you are saying how you feel, and the other person is hearing what he wants to hear about how you feel. The only thing that is really going on is you expressing your mind. So when I suggest that you pay attention to the way you are communicating, I am specifically referring to the frame of mind you are currently in while the communication is taking place. If you are in a frame of mind that conveys anger or fear of any nature, then that is all that will be perceived by the person who is hearing—the words will be superfluous. If you are coming from a place of peace and trust, even though there is no apparent reason to extend trust, then trust will be perceived and true communication will take place. I would suggest that as I use the phrase, "extend trust from your state of mind," you have the awareness and the recognition that what you are extending trust into is the truer nature of the Being with whom you are communicating. And then allow that trust to resonate with that person from his own sense of consciousness into what you may perceive as a more limited frame of consciousness.

An Image Given:

> *There are two cartoon characters communicating with each other. There are talk balloons going away from their mouths filled with words, and then just above each of the two characters is an extension or spirit outline of that person and there are also talk balloons extending from them up there where the real communication is happening. As the words are exchanged by the lower figures, they are just words; the thought and the trusting that you are really communicating in peace is flowing from the upper image in heart shaped balloons, being received there and then filtering down below and being understood.*

This will take a little practice, will it not? It is very difficult to change a pattern in which you have invested a great deal of validity. My suggestion would be to look back upon the success of that pattern in the communication process, and I would say if it has worked, stick with it. If it hasn't, perhaps it's time to try something new.

How do I resolve a financial disagreement I'm involved in with this kind of communication?

Another Image Given:

> *There is a little dinghy boat, with you on one side of it and someone else on the other side, and you are pulling on the sides of this boat, each of you feeling that it's your boat, and the boat just splits in two, right down the keel.*

There is another matter here, one of recognizing value. I am saying be very clear as to what you value. Because it is this lack of clarity in the values which are foremost in your mind that are creating the fears over the outcome of the disposition of the property. There are relationships involved and that old demon, money, is involved. What I would like to have you consider is that, in the reality of it, there is only one value that is truly involved and that is the value that you place upon your peace of mind. The illustration of the boat being torn in two was to illustrate that when your mind is torn, nothing of value comes about as a result. Nothing that is apparently earned at the price of your peace of mind will truly have any lasting value to you, and you will recognize this quite clearly after the fact.

I am suggesting that you take some time to be very quiet, to look within your mind and play the scenario out in every conceivable way that you think it may occur, both in the ways you would like to see it happen and in the ways that you are afraid that it might happen. Be aware of the sense of peace—I could refer to it as a sense of satisfaction, of total satisfaction—that occurs with each scenario that you unfold. Then take the one which is totally satisfying to you, and hold it. Hold it gently, hold it without fear, and allow it to happen. Trust that it will happen. And please try to avoid any attachment of fear between the time you let go of it and the time that it becomes manifest, because the process will change if the thoughts within your mind change. You must allow it to go in complete freedom, unencumbered and unaccompanied by any later, "I wonder was that really right? Will it really turn out that way?" No future attachments of fear. Unencumbered. Allow it to be. *If it left your mind in absolute clarity and remains in that state, it will be so.*

Liken this, if you will, to the night dreams you have within this waking dream. You are very well aware that you can make anything happen that you want simply by the pattern of your thoughts that exists while you are sleeping. Yet the activity changes within the night dream as your thought within that dream changes, and that is what I am explaining to you happens within the bigger waking dream. Have you ever had a night dream where you were chased by a tiger and you were in absolute panic and fear, and then had an inkling that said, "Wait a moment . . . I must be dreaming." And you turned around, and the tiger was gone. You simply allowed your tiger to be gone.

Choose what you value most. If you choose peace, then that is what you will have in whatever form you decide to have it. Please do not accept this as an esoteric explanation. I am giving you as real information as is possible for you to have and still remain dreaming. It is the information that will ultimately help you to see that you are dreaming and establish a greater willingness to wake up. You will either seek and find validations to confirm the dream or validations to let go of the dream and that, too, is a choice.

What if people want different outcomes from the same issue?

The outcome of any situation is determined by the motivation behind the thought which caused the situation. When you choose for peace and joy for both you and your brother, that will be the outcome regardless of other circumstances. Because you are always one with each other, you will accommodate each others' true desire. This does not now appear to be the case because you both typically see your desires and interests conflicting, and so you give conflicting meaning to your thoughts which must produce a conflicted outcome. To change that outcome, you must want for him what you want for yourself.

I remind you that physical experiences serve only to identify the thought processes which reflect your beliefs. The object around which the conflict is occurring could take the form of anything which has value to you. But to see it as being the reason for or source of the conflict misses the point. Your conflicting desires of outcome reflect your belief in scarcity. Ask yourself if this issue in conflict would even exist if you knew of a certainty that you could bring anything into your experience that you chose to have there.

Do I understand you to say that when there are opposing viewpoints and you choose then to have peace, the issue will be resolved to the benefit of both?

When you choose peace, the ultimate benefit that will be derived is your receiving peace. You will come to recognize that it is the only thing that has value and is worth choosing. Allow your brother's benefit to take whatever form he has chosen to receive it in.

How long will it take to reach this state?

That one is entirely up to you. Please understand that the moment you wholly choose peace, the experience of peace is instantaneous. The process of your creating the thought patterns of continuously, unequivocally choosing peace in each and every situation will take as long as you choose. *The reason to choose peace is that it is not of the illusion. It is a reflection of Reality.* Choices made that do not bring you peace appear to validate the illusion and keep your attention anchored in it.

Peace Through Doing

I recently had an experience in which I was in a certain space or feeling within me that lasted the whole day.

There was no doubt or fear there. How do I get back into that space consciously?

I call your attention to the fact that on this day, you were in a state of non-thinking. You were in a state of feeling. It is the thinking part that generates the doubts and the fears. When you are in a state of feeling, you are most closely aligned to your state of Being. Very often, this is thought to be a most difficult process and state of mind to put yourself into because, after all, you have described yourself as a thinking being. Thinking has become a process which is mistakenly believed to be synonymous with knowing, and I will reinforce to you that this is upside-down knowledge. Knowing comes to you as you step back past your ego's perception.

The feeling of this can be most easily achieved for you through your love of what you do. It is the process of losing your thinking patterns in the process of doing something that brings you peace. So it is not "doing" as you might describe it which encompasses the acts of thinking and planning. In your case, it is the doing of that which you love which releases the need to think and, therefore, opens up the process of being able to clearly feel. The feeling comes to you because of the love that is generated by what you are doing.

"Doing" has become a bad word because it generally has been associated with willfulness. The doing as I am describing it to you now is more aptly described as willingness . . . a willingness to surrender yourself to a feeling of self-acceptance which is achieved through the simple act of loving what you are doing.

The Importance of Feelings

As you fill your lives from day to day and hour to hour with words and deeds, I would suggest that many times you overlook the feelings that accompany the words and the deeds. Often the feelings are uncomfortable, generating fear and apprehension. I would suggest they are still well worth paying attention to, because it is the habit of learning to be in touch with those feelings that opens the door to the truer feelings, those of peace and joy, the feelings that ultimately bring us into our awareness of Being, of being the true extension of God.

It will also be in your paying attention to the feelings that do generate fear, that you will find it easier to let go of them as you compare them to the feelings of peace. I could speak to you in volumes about how to let go of fear, of why to let go of fear, of the unreality of fear, but it would be rare if any of these words really captured your attention. It will be the *feeling* of peace; it will be your experience of being in the space of knowing that you are well entrenched in the Mind of God where there is no fear that will then make if far easier for you to discredit the feelings of fear which are generated when you forget who you are.

So my suggestion is simply this: surrender to your feeling, whatever it may be. Surrender to it because it will be your closest communication to the Being of your Self.

Which come first, feelings or thought?

You would expect a feeling to be generated by a thought. But to describe more appropriately what has been happening, a feeling has been preexistent, and it has been the feeling—more than likely one that you are quite unconscious of—which has generated the thought that then seems to produce a responding feeling. But it has indeed, been the feeling that has first been present.

Let me try to clarify it more by telling it to you like this: When you are in a general frame of mind of being at peace, when your feelings are ones of joy and love and harmony, then do you not find that your thoughts are always those which encompass, or seem to be extended from, this base of feeling? The feelings that appear to be generated subsequently as a result of those thoughts of peace and love and harmony are a continuation of the original feeling from which the thought was formed.

You will also discover, as you reach the point of being more consistently in a frame of mind that resonates only to peace, that the "thoughts" and feelings are inseparable, and it would not be meaningful for you to even wonder which came first.

I point out this distinction to you at this time because, generally speaking, the thoughts that you are now most accustomed to are those that are generated from an ego response to a feeling of fear. And in that regard, it is more appropriate to be aware that your feelings are "the prime mover," so to speak. As we have spoken about practicing being in touch with those feelings, you will notice that the feelings that seem to generate fear are most easily let go of as you allow yourself to place them in *comparison* to the feelings of peace. If you were to try to let go of your feelings of fear by thoughts of peace, you would find it far more difficult.

I am speaking to you now from the standpoint of circumventing the ego by being aware of your feelings and being aware of the thoughts that they produce.

Be Gentle With Yourself

When I am in that ego state of seeing my brother's mistakes, and I'm not willing to make that shift to seeing his perfection, what is the most helpful thing I can do at this point?

To be absolutely aware that the unwillingness is not changing you. Because of your past patterns of understanding, you would believe that as you do not allow yourself to be perfect, there must be some type of retribution, you must in some way suffer to pay for your sins. You are now coming to an understanding that tells you that this is not true. Stay with this feeling.

It is impossible for you to change your true Self. It is only possible for you to either recognize that Self or continue to recognize a limited perception of that Self which we have described as being the ego. The entire process becomes one of satisfying the ego by attempting to live up to its demands that you be as "spiritual" now as you feel you should be. Know that as you seek yourself spiritually, your ego will appear to aid you in that quest.

There is something here that would be helpful for you to be aware of and that is not to be judgmental about your ego. Do not put your attention in any way on what you may consider to be negative influence or negative impact upon you by your ego. For as you allow that attention to rest upon your ego, you will strengthen it. You will come to think of it as being an evil aspect of yourself, but it is not. Your ego is simply a misperception that you hold about yourself, and that does not make it evil.

The kindliest, most helpful thing that you may participate in as you find yourself in the position that you have described is simply this: acknowledge to yourself that this is, in fact, your perception at this moment and let it go. Do not resist it; do not condemn yourself for it. Feel grateful that you are in a position to step back momentarily and observe what is happening. Acknowledge the presence of your ego, and acknowledge the Presence of your Being as well. It will be the acknowledgment that you make of the Presence of your Being that will allow you to refocus and reestablish the feeling of peace.

Being judgmental about yourself when you feel that you are in a state of mind that is less than what you want to be can only encourage that state of mind to have a value to you. Therefore, it will be with you to a far greater degree than what you would anticipate. It will continue to grow as you continue to give attention to it, as you continue to be judgmental of it.

You are learning that Love has no opposite. Therefore, what would it mean to you if you could simply be in a state of love about whatever it is that happens to be in your mind at the moment, including being judgmental about yourself and seeing yourself as being totally immersed within your ego? Could you still be in a state of love with yourself? If there is no opposite to Love, what would be of greater benefit to help you dissolve anything that apparently was in conflict with love? To love your ego would not sound like a logical approach, would it—to love yourself when you felt yourself being hateful? But that is precisely what I am suggesting.

I am suggesting that to begin to change those patterns of being judgmental, you not concentrate on making any change at all, but rather allow yourself to be aware that you truly exist in a state of Love. Allow that state to become more clear to you, and as you do, you will begin to build a pattern of becoming loving in all circumstances and situations. The other patterns will begin to drop away. You will do nothing to attempt to change the other patterns.

You will simply replace in your thinking the thoughts that were less loving with thoughts that are more loving.

I could not at any time suggest to you that the most expedient way of becoming less judgmental would be to exercise the opposite to that pattern because I would be advising you to put more of your attention into the process of judging. As you would put more attention into that, you would find it increasingly difficult to let go of it. *It is impossible to practice being non-judgmental.*

Being in a state of peace will bring you joy. Being in a state of joy will allow you to see your own loving nature. By the same premise, I cannot tell you to practice being peaceful. What I can suggest to you is to let go of thoughts that are not peaceful. That's all, just let go. You let go of them by not judging them. You let go of them by not resisting them. You let go of them by firmly understanding they have no value to you. They do not change you. Peace comes of its own accord when you have made this choice for it.

Will the process of letting go be quickened if we ask the Holy Spirit to help us in letting go of the old thought patterns?

The answer most emphatically is, yes! I would, however, like to suggest to you that you not concern yourself with how quickly something may or may not happen. That will encourage you to inappropriately focus your attention on having an expectation as to how the process is going to work and if it is working effectively within the parameters that you have set for it. Instead, trust. Trust that it is working perfectly and in whatever time it takes, trust that this is part of the perfection that is happening at the moment. The principle again is this: when you allow your attention to inappropriately focus on this thing that we will now call "time," then you have identified the importance that time holds for you. You have presumed that there will never be enough of it because if this does not happen quickly enough, then you must move onto something else because you certainly only have a limited amount of time.

You see, this whole process becomes one of changing your mind about limitation. And I will tell you that your making of time is the greatest limitation you have created. As you see yourself being a prisoner of this world, you will forever be a prisoner here. As you allow the Holy Spirit to work with you, to release you from all of the bonds, you must trust it will happen in whatever way that will best serve you. It will not be in your conscious awareness or determination of what that best way is. It will be by trust. I will tell you now, there is no place for you to go anyway, so what's the rush?

As you have heard in the past, it is most helpful for you to keep your attention focused only in the moment. This has become a concept, but has not been understood. Keeping your attention focused in the moment will shift your awareness to an understanding that it is only this moment that truly exists. This cannot be understood when you try to make it applicable within the framework of your world as you know it now, because you will readily understand that this is not the way your world works. So part of the trust is giving up the notion of the way you see your world working and relying upon the Holy Spirit to show you a different Vision.

You will not find a justification for what I suggest as you look around you. You will only find it inside you, in that place of Knowing that needs no validation from the outside world. But you cannot find that moment when you seek it, believing that you only have a limited amount of time to spend seeking it. Don't you see?

That is always the dichotomy that appears to present itself in this process of waking up. It is the parameters that our ego will allow us to employ which apparently limit our spiritual visibility.

You have chosen to experience your Self, and as long as you allow your attention to confirm this, then you must understand that whatever is happening to you, for you and around you, is happening to bring this about, and it is happening in a state of absolute perfection. When this is forgotten, this whole business of spiritually Awakening becomes a very arduous task and is not much fun. Where is the joy? Where has the joy gone when you must condemn yourself for not Awakening?

I will tell you again, you are already Awake. You have, in truth, never stopped being Awake; you have never stopped being less than the perfection in which you were created. It is only your refusal to accept this idea that keeps you from the experience of it. Attempting to change yourself instead of accepting yourself gives your ego another path to pursue and will only perpetuate that entire process. It will also perpetuate unhappiness and disappointment.

Allow yourself to be in a state of joy and know that when you are in that state, you are in a state of God. The rest will happen. When you are in a state of joy, then disappointment falls away. You did nothing to make it go away. But there will always be this voice that says, "There is no logical reason for me to be joyful when I have debts, when I have things around me that are keeping me from being joyful. When my husband doesn't understand me, when my mother-in-law thinks I am less than the perfect wife, when my friends judge me wrongly, when I cannot pay the electric bill, how can I be joyful?" And it is obviously less than logical when I say to you that being in a state of joy is the only thing that will change those things that you see around you. *It is not those things going away that will allow you to be in a state of joy.* It is your making the choice for joy and for peace that will create your thinking patterns that will reflect joy and peace.

When your mind is in a state of perfect and perpetual peace, it will be quite impossible for you to have any experience that is not reflective of perpetual peace and joy and love. Changing the inner script will change the outer play.

It Doesn't Matter What You Do

In the last year, I have been feeling a conflict with continuing to do my volunteer work, and at the same time part of me seems to be saying I shouldn't be a quitter but should finish what I've started. If I do quit the volunteer work and there is a void, will the universe fill the void for me?

Let me say two things: First, I will attempt to eliminate a lot of the mystery that surrounds the question, "What shall I do? What are the things that I may do that will bring me closer to the realization and recognition of my peace within and ultimately to the discovery and remembrance of myself?" And I will say to you, it is totally immaterial what you do. It matters not. Please hear me and dwell upon this.

It does not matter what you do. The significance of anything you attach yourself to is the why of your doing it.

We will return once again to the premise that there is nothing happening in your world except that which is expressive and reflective of your thinking process at any given moment. Should you elect to work with any group, do so. Do so and ask yourself why you are there. What is it you are trying to discover that you are trying to teach yourself through this experience?

Allow whatever that choice may be to become the lesson. The task will be unimportant; why you are doing it will mean everything. As you come to a closer alignment with this understanding, you will ultimately know that you may choose any task, or you may choose no task, and the result will be exactly the same.

But again, I suggest that you do not stand in judgment of yourself or think that one method is better or more spiritually advanced than another. Be where you are every moment. Honor where you are every moment. Do not stand in judgment or resist anything that seems to come to your mind, or presents itself to you as either a challenge or a positive or negative experience. Stand before it and ask the Holy Spirit to help you understand why. You may pick any situation that you like to bring you the understanding of whatever lesson it is that you have decided to learn, or merely an experience you have decided to have.

I will tell you that the choices you have made to this point have been made with the understanding that by changing the environment around you, you will be making the world a better place for yourself and for others. As a motive, this is quite laudable. But as a teaching device, it is ineffectual because you are asking the event to teach you as opposed to allowing the answer to come from within yourself and merely be illustrated through the event. You see, it is a very subtle difference. On the one hand, you are focusing your attention on the event as being the answer, and on the other, you are focusing your attention inward and recognizing yourself to be the answer. But the event does not change.

How many times have we spoken that the world does not change; only your perception of it does. And how does your perception change? It changes as you change your mind about yourself and the world then appears to change. There is nothing in the world that is not made and not put there as a result of your thinking.

A change of attitude will change your experience. So to answer your question directly, I must say to you, become more tuned in as to what it is that you are seeking. Ask. Always ask. It will be in the asking that you will bring to your conscious attention the answer that you are seeking. I have said before, many questions are answered but are not heard. You will not hear the answer until you have opened your mind to it. You open your mind to it by clearly defining what it is that you seek to know.

Your ego at that point will attempt to quickly outline the limiting parameters within which it will allow the answer to become apparent to you. It will do so based upon your past judgments of what these experiences have meant to you; but of course, that is what you are seeking to change. So I would only suggest to you that you allow yourself to be open to hearing whatever the answer may be, even though it may be presented to you in quite a different fashion than what you have experienced before.

I would like to give you a small hint: Many times you will wonder whether or not you have received an answer. You will ask the question and then say, "Is this the answer that I am to hear?" And you will wonder whether or not this is another dictate of your ego or if you have, indeed, heard the Voice of your whole Self. To know the difference ask, "Within this answer, have I become more loving? Have I become more peaceful? Do I find joy here?" That is, incidentally, only one question because the three are the same. You will know, based upon these criteria, whether the answer has come from the totality of your Self, or from your limited self.

Guards to the Gate of Peace

As a mother I have so much guilt surrounding this question. I have a son I was not prepared to have, and

I am on a very different wave length from his father in how we perceive the world. Would I be doing the right thing by leaving and creating what I would like to have around me, or am I meant to stay and be responsible for the situation? If I do leave, will I ruin a little person's life?

Let me say to you first: you have but one responsibility and that is to be your Self, to express the love and the peace and the joy that is the definition of you. There is no one around you now, nor will there ever be anyone around you who will settle for less, regardless of what the conscious or apparent expression of their desires may be.

The little one bears most heavily upon your mind, so allow me to say this. He seeks for love and the love that you have to give to him cannot be recognized even by you until you feel it for yourself. As you seek for love and to find the expression of your true Being, you aid in his seeking as well. It is only through the recognition of your Self and your experiencing it that you will, in any meaningful way: pass it on.

I will tell you that guilt and judgment are guards to the gate of peace. As long as you present yourself before them, there will be no way for you to pass through. But I also ask you to understand that being on the fear side of that gate to peace will bring no one happiness or joy or any expression that is in any way vaguely recognizable as being that which they truly seek. So when I say to you, "Seek your peace, seek your Self-expression first," I am not advocating or offering you an opportunity to judge yourself as being guilty because you have placed yourself in a position which you perceive as being ahead of your child.

You see, it is quite the contrary. If you do not first place yourself in this position of peace, then you have given the child no position at all.

Once you have begun this realignment of your thinking, there will be another phenomenon which you will begin to become aware of, and that is of the participation of your child. I will tell you that the child is more aware of what is going on than he is able to express. You cannot see this, because you are in a position of being unclear about your own expression.

I will not advocate to you to stay in or to leave the relationship you are in. What I will advocate to you is to direct your attention to your own well-being. And if you will pay attention to your well-being, then what happens within the relationship will simply be of a natural effect. It will take the course that best serves the development of your Self and his Self.

Chapter Three

Experiencing Your Thoughts

"When you are in touch with your natural state of Being, when you are in a feeling of harmonious peace and requests are made from this state, there is only one way for you to experience the results. When your mind is in a state of confusion and a state of fear, the only way for you to experience what is made manifest by those fears is in a fearful fashion."

The Mind/Experience Relationship

When turmoil or chaos appears in your mind, it will be experienced as a form of confusion and chaos outside your mind. You do not make unpleasant or uncomfortable circumstances to teach yourself lessons. When there is a lack of clarity within your thought patterns, that lack of clarity will be reflected in the form of a chaotic life. The true process is one where the ego receives information as to the confusion that exists and translates that confusion as not being able to control the outcome which becomes an unknown and, therefore, fearful. And, as your attention is focused on these fears, they will become manifest.

The message your ego allows you to receive from what I have just described will be quite different. It will say that once again, you have made something bad; something you have interpreted as negative. This serves its purpose very well, because it continues to keep your mind in a state of confusion and gives you the excuse to feel that there is something for you to do to straighten out the confusion.

This type of thinking also leads you along another path which is not helpful: this is the one that tells you that something is controlling your life that is beyond your conscious ability to affect. This can come to you in two forms: believing that there is another force of any type that has control over your life and that makes decisions for you, or believing that the information can come from your subconscious mind, which you feel is also beyond your level of understanding and, therefore, beyond your control. I will tell you that neither of these is true.

What appear to you to be the thought processes of your subconscious mind appear so because you are unwilling to be in touch with them. These thoughts or issues lie clearly within your conscious mind, but they have been there in a form unrecognized by you. In this lack of recognition lies the basis for confusion. It is this confusion that leads to the manifestation of your fears.

Once again, the process works like this: There is confusion in your mind. This is interpreted as being out of control which creates fear. Once your attention has been directed to those fears, they will manifest in your life because they have become real in your mind. *It is not possible for you to experience anything in your physical life that is not encompassed within your thought patterns.*

Now, your ego will take this statement and attempt to make you a prisoner of it. It will attempt to make feelings of guilt, saying to you, "Now see what you have done! Now see what a pretty mess you have made." Do not listen to this information. Hear instead the truer implication of what I am saying. Know with utmost certainty that the statement "nothing comes to you that is not held in your mind" is an offer of total freedom. You do have the power to determine what will be in your mind.

The question for you now arises, how then does this fit with prior information I have been given which says, "Try to empty your mind, try to free your mind from fearful thought patterns." I will tell you that this message has as its specific meaning to give up the thought patterns that have been made by your ego mind, by your mind that has within it a sense of limitation based upon prior experience—"old tapes"—as you would put it. My encouragement is to allow yourself to open your mind to peace, to the peaceful attitude you have that reflects more accurately your natural state of Mind, the state of Mind that reflects your Being. It is in this peaceful state that you will experience clarity and you will experience the absolute certainty that when you create an experience in your physical life from this state of peace, there will be no confusion as to its outcome.

There is no force outside of you that has any validity upon the Reality of your Being, or that would bring to you what you have called "lessons" of any nature which would be experienced by you as less than pleasant. When you have, however, developed a state of thinking that believes lessons learned are, for the most part, unpleasant experiences, then you will bring those lessons to yourself to be experienced in this way. Allow me to remind you that this mode of thinking is one that has been developed over eons of time during which you have convinced yourself that you are a guilty and unworthy person and are not entitled to receive the experience of love that is yours as the Presence of your Being.

As you allow yourself to reside more consistently in a peaceful state, the truth of this will become known to you. Let me put it another way: when you are in touch with your natural state of Being, when you are in a feeling of harmonious peace and requests are made from this state, there is only one way for you to experience the results. Likewise, when your mind is in a state of confusion and a state of fear, the only way for you to experience what is made manifest by those fears is in a fearful fashion. In its most simplistic form you may think of it like this: chaos in; chaos out, peace in; peace out, love within; love without.

The meaning of what I am telling you is becoming more apparent. There is nothing that happens to you; there are only the thought processes and patterns of the state of mind in which you exist. That constitutes the sum total of it. What you experience as your physical reality is only a confirmation of what you are experiencing in your mind. And as you go through this Awakening process, you will discover that it is not even necessary for the physical confirmation. All that is happening to you is happening in your mind.

Should you continue to experience any unpleasantness in your physical existence, then know that there has been a value placed by your ego on these experiences. And once again, rather than judging yourself as being bad because you have allowed these to happen, see them as a reflection of what is going on in your mind, and choose again. Therein lies your freedom! Choose again, and again, and again and again until the process of your choosing becomes one of normally, naturally wanting to choose peace.

Now, there is another thing that is troubling you which is, "How can I choose peace, how can I consistently put these choices into effect in my mind when apparently my mind, my thinking, my life is so influenced by other lives around me?" Allow me to assure you that this is another ploy of your ego to reinforce that your existing patterns can not possibly be changed unless all the other people's patterns around you conform to your way of thinking. And I will tell you, this is upside down. The truth is it will not be seen by you that any other patterns of thinking around you are changing until you have changed your own. It is in your thinking processes that you have perceived the ego focus which seems to be apparently taking place in those around you.

When I say you will only experience that which resides in your mind, I do not say this is true with the exclusion of how you would experience the effects of someone else's activities. There are no exceptions to this principle. As difficult as this will be for you to believe and understand, I will tell you this: when your mind resides in a state of total peace, when it is impossible for you to experience anything other than peace, you will see everyone around you existing within that same peaceful state. I do not offer this to you as an intellectual exercise in trying to understand how this would happen. I offer it to you simply as a statement of truth.

In your particular place of thinking at this moment, the primary value in having the physical experience is to show you what is happening within your mind. As you see something seemingly taking place in your life, see it as an opportunity to know what is happening in your mind.

When you experience harmony and peace and boundless joy, know that your mind is in a state of reflecting a truer perception of your Reality. When you experience fear or lack of any kind, simply know that is what is in your limited mind. Do not judge yourself for this; it is not even necessary to know why it is there. It is enough to know of its residence and to know with equal certainty you have the opportunity to choose for it not to be there.

The truth of this could not be more simple. I recognize the practical application of your consistently choosing to have this unqualified peace is not perceived by you as being a simple process. But please do not confuse the simplicity of the truth with what you may experience as difficulty in implementing it. Do not be misled by your ego as you attempt to choose peace. When you do not see it manifest, don't say, "There must be something more complex that I am not understanding," for indeed, there is not. The complexity lies only in the implementation of what I am telling you.

I know that some of you have also had the feeling of needing to pull yourself out of a financial rut and have indeed been attempting many things to accomplish this. And when they do not seem to work, you ask yourself if perhaps there is something different that you should be doing; perhaps there is another path, a better way. To apply the principles of which I have just been speaking, I would suggest you approach it with an understanding that it is not what you do that will achieve the purpose that you desire. It is the frame of mind within which you find yourself that will be the difference.

You have approached your many tasks with the thought system, the belief, that the harder you work, the greater will be your reward. This belief is based upon an historical reference of what you perceive as having been taught to you through prior experience. This is an incorrect perception. If you will examine it, however, you will see that it has illustrated to you the very point that I was describing earlier; because you have first made a belief of this, it has therefore become a reality for you. In your current circumstances, the fear that is resident and accompanying this belief system has imposed the limitations which you are experiencing. How many times recently have you said to yourself, "No matter how much I do, it doesn't seem to work!" Your saying that is a description and an expression of the thought pattern which I am describing, and it is that thought pattern that is proving itself to you by not working. It is what you are experiencing that is simply a confirmation of what your are thinking.

Manifesting physical needs can be perceived and experienced in as limited or as limitless a frame of reference as you hold in your mind as being the appropriate expression of your Being. When you give any form of limitation to it, then it will be limited. When you perceive it as being unable to work, then it will not work. When you remove your sense of limitation, then you will experience it as being limitless.

The only boundary that exists to an experience of any nature is the boundary that exists within your frame of thinking at the time that you shape it. So when your motive becomes to experience your Self, you will experience it without limit simply because that is the only true description of you: a Being without limit.

To try to understand how all this works at this moment would only be an additional excuse for your intellect to enter the picture. What

I am telling you at this moment will not register with your logical, rational mind. But as you release the boundaries within which that logical, rational mind holds you, then you will create the space for the recognition of the truth to resonate within you.

Your ego would have you believe that it will become increasingly easy for you to experience your spiritual or enlightened Self as you are able to relieve the fiscal responsibility and become more peaceful, and this too, is backwards. Choose to be within a state of peace. With assurance, choose to have your financial problems solved. It will be done and in a way that brings peace and happiness, harmony and joy into your awareness.

You cannot be joyful because you have solved a problem that has come into your awareness. This would only confirm to you that it is possible for other problems to come into your awareness which you would then have to go through the process of solving to bring you additional joy. When you recognize your Self as being the Presence of joy, you will know that there are no problems that accompany it. Problems are not reflective of a joyful mind. So let's keep the horse in front of the cart. Attention directed toward the memory of your Self does not promote fearful thinking.

You have but one choice to make and that is to either continue seeing through the blinders and veils of past perception, or to start anew. I would encourage you to begin this new process with the expectation that you have requested truth, and truth will come to you. It will come as rapidly as you create the space to enable yourself to hear it. So I ask you to begin the process now. Do not attempt to understand what I am saying. Simply say to yourself, "I choose peace instead of this." Allow yourself to feel the accompanying warmth of the Love that envelopes you as you recognize the Presence of the peace you have chosen. Recognize your Self in this space and the rest will be known to you.

The Power of the Mind

Given a situation where one has developed a successful life with position, wealth, and material possessions, and then that suddenly changes and all these things are lost under great duress and stress, what is going on from a spiritual perspective? Is the whole Self reprogramming for different values?

It is well to understand that nothing truly ever comes to you that is beyond your conscious available mind. Were this not to be true, then you would still have the feeling that things could be done to you. If either your whole Self, as you currently view it, or your subconscious mind which is beyond your conscious reach, were to be directing your activities, then it would still appear to you to be something bringing events into your life over which you had no control. And this would totally violate the principle I have given you before that is: you will experience what you see first within your mind. What is in your mind will make its appearance in your physical world. So you see, if something were in your unconscious mind, or even what you could accept as being a part of your Mind—if, in your conscious attitude, it was beyond your control, then you could be a victim of your Self which is no different that being a victim of any other circumstances. This is not a belief that is helpful for you to hold.

What I am attempting to explain, however, is that there is much in your conscious mind that you have not sorted out, but which is there within reach and within understanding. However, it appears to be a blur. I refer to it as being a feeling of chaos. This chaos would be a thousand jumbled thoughts not clearly distinguishable in your conscious perception. And when that becomes the case, because you are experiencing in your physical world a reflection of what is inside your mind, you will experience that chaos. As your mind lacks clarity, then those circumstances that you are manifesting in your physical world will equally lack clarity.

As your experiences begin to take a shape which appear to be of their own making, and you sense yourself losing control of the situation outside your mind, you have obviously lost control of circumstances within your mind. It appears that things are happening to you, and your mind will then immediately jump to a fear of loss of whatever it is at that moment that you have the greatest fear of losing. Because you see things going beyond control, you will first want to guard those things which you consider to be most precious. As that feeling of needing to guard them arises, it comes from a point of view of fear. And when the fear of loss becomes real in your mind, it becomes physically manifest.

Now, as is the case in most other things that you experience, this concept itself can become frightening—that if you allow your mind to feel fear, then those things which are most representational of fear in your outside world will appear. Your ego loves to think in terms that are to you negative, those things which will bring adverse impact. But think with me for a moment of how wonderful this concept truly is because it should be saying to you, "When peace is in my mind, when Love is in my mind, then that is what I will experience."

How many times have we said, "Choose peace." I will assure you that when you choose peace, it is not simply because your environment will reflect peacefulness, but I would also encourage you to understand that it is more closely reflecting the natural state of your Being. And this, after all, is the name of the game.

Would the environment as well be experienced as peaceful?

Of course.

In the midst of war?

Get to the cause of war. Don't try to go through the intellectual and mental exercises that say, "I can be at peace in the midst of war." Understand why war is created. When you no longer accept conflict as being real or having value, there will be no reason for it being in your thoughts. And if it is not in your thoughts, there is no possible way for it to appear in your physical experience. I will not try to tell you that it is impossible for your mind to find a semblance of peace in the midst of war because indeed, it is possible. But it is not the fullest experience of peace, for here no sense of conflict would be possible.

The phrase, "Yea, though I walk through the valley of death I shall fear no evil"—is that a metaphor for what you were describing?

Indeed, it is. The metaphor there would be more clearly stated, "Though I seem to exist in a state of illusion, I will have no fear when I recognize it is, in fact, an illusion. Yea, though I walk through it, yea, though I seem to be in a place I am not, I will fear no evil because I recognize that I am dreaming and have truly never left my peaceful home."

The way out of the chaos of our mind then is, as you have already explained, to choose peace.

Choose peace. Above all, choose peace until it becomes recognized that it is the only choice. And when the light of that eventually dawns upon you, suddenly you will Awaken and recognize that you have never left peace. Then you will understand completely the meaning of the word "illusion".

I have no more questions unless you would like to give more information.

There are volumes of information. There have been volumes of information already given, but only that which you are at the point of accepting is worthwhile. Therefore, we will wait until you have additional questions which will reflect that you are at the point of accepting.

Choices in Manifesting

There is a great deal of confusion in your minds about how the actual mechanical effects are achieved in what you call "manifesting." It is what I have spoken about before as, you will experience what you choose to see. Because you are already a totally perfect Being with no real sense of lack, for you to believe that you manifest material crutches, if you will, is for you to believe that you need those crutches. If, on the other hand, you are able to retain the recognition of the truth of your Self, and you set about this business of manifesting, do you see how you would approach it differently? You would then be seeing it from the standpoint of not having fear or need attached to it. You would see it simply become another piece in the game you have chosen to play. Another toy. You may have anything in this physical realm that you choose to have. I've said this before but it has never quite settled into a sense of knowledge.

The term "abundant universe" is an ego term if it refers to anything that comes to you because you have requested it from a feeling of need. The term "infinite universe" is more accurate because it helps you to reflect in your consciousness the awareness that an infinite universe really refers to the Mind of God. To believe that within the Mind of God abundance exists also creates the thought that there could be a lack. Abundance is a word that has an opposite. And opposites do not exist in the Mind of God.

Within the framework of the physical experience, you may create as much abundance as you desire. It is well, however, for you to recognize that this type of abundance has no connection to, and is not sponsored by, the Mind of God. What is valuable here for you to see is that this ability you have to create this abundance, even within the physical dimension, stems from your true creative capacities as an infinite Being. In the state of true Reality of who and what you are, your creative capabilities would be expressed very differently. But because nothing is withheld from you in this state of dreaming, you may also use this creative capacity in any fashion that you wish. If you wish it to make sickness to prove a point to you, then indeed, you will make sickness. If you use it to make abundance of any sort, then I would ask you to understand that it is also you who are making that abundance.

You have probably noticed that on occasion when you have attempted to make financial abundance or things for you to have within the physical experience, it will be accompanied by the thought that you are not deserving to have those things. I'd like to explain to you that this thought is not quite accurate. If you listen to it from the ego's reference, then it could well be that the ego is trying to keep you in this state of confusion by telling you that you can't really have this. And that if you attempt to have it and you don't get it, then you will simply appear to be proving the ego's point that you are not worthy of it.

What I am referring to here is another thought that will be in your mind as you try to create or manifest anything that you would term to be "abundant" while it still is accompanied by this nagging feeling that it is not quite right. That nagging feeling is your sense of the value of the abundance. And this is what I would ask you to change your awareness of. Allow yourself to lift the identification of this abundance as having value. If you wish to have something simply as a part of the experience of the physical dimension, understand clearly that you may have it. Understand also that the only value that you can appropriately attach to the knowledge of your ability to bring it about is that it ties very closely to your true creative ability which is the expression of who you Are. The thing itself that will be manifest in your physical consciousness has no value. But the fact that you can manifest or make it, and that this manifestation bears a parallel to the true expression of your Being, does have value.

I will also tell you that while the ego, in struggling to maintain a sense of importance to your identity, would, on the one hand, tell you that you do not deserve to have abundance manifest in your life, it could also, on the other hand, as you come into the full recognition of what the true meaning of manifesting is, turn completely around and tell you, "Ah, you see how wonderful it is because 'we' were able to do this!" To listen to either message would substantiate your sense of limitation, and that sense of limitation will be validated if you value the thing that you manifest. But if what you allow to happen is the recognition that the ability to manifest is nothing more than a parallel to the creative extension of your Being, then it takes on a totally different light.

When we are not in a state of limitation, are all our needs instantaneously met?

When you are fully Awakened, the word "need" is not even part of your vocabulary; there is only the recognition of fullness and wholeness. I would like to make something else clear here as well. This state of mind of limitation exists whether you are perceiving yourself as being a physical body or as being a spirit body. You are Mind, but as long as that Mind has any sense of limitation to it, then you will not experience the totality of your Being. Existence in physical form, however, presents you with the most radical departure from the concept of being Mind.

Should you become fully Awakened and still wish to retain a physical form, you would not simply cast off the perceived needs to support that form. Those would not disappear, because they are inherent in the arena of physical form. However, should you make this choice, you would realize very quickly what we have just discussed, which is that it would be quite easy for you to manifest whatever chosen need there was of either the physical form or the thing that you manifested to support it. These things would simply become by-products to being in the physical experience. And what I was relating to you before was that in the process of waking up, the same thing holds true. Manifest whatever you like, but recognize the difference.

We have spoken many times about the value of recognizing motivation, and I hope this serves to further clarify the meaning. One brings you from the point of view of need which serves to misdirect your attention from the real issue, while the other allows the real issue, which is your Awakening, to be fully resonant with you, to be fully resident within you as well. And then all other things that you attempt to bring into your conscious awareness within your physical experience are simply things that are desired to support that physical experience, but do not have a basis in Reality.

No one else, no other force in the universe, will support your call for manifestation, simply because every other force that exists within the universe that is in alignment with the recognition of the Mind of God sees no need. I am not trying to tell you here to abandon your need, only your definition of it. See it as a mechanism to support the physical experience and then do whatever you like with it.

Let me add one more thing in case it isn't clear yet. The ego can send you on many wild goose chases with the belief that the choices you make have value attached to them regarding your being able to wake up. Please understand, these are diversions. They are only attempts by the ego to cloud your thinking from the single issue that is at hand. If you can hold this awareness and simply allow each choice as it appears to come with the full recognition that it doesn't matter, you then can choose whatever it is you prefer. The significance is for you to understand that whatever choice you make simply needs to be made from the basis of recognition of your Being. This is what I have been referring to as making a choice that gives you a sense of peace. That sense of peace is the closest recognition that you currently have of being in alignment with your Self. The choices themselves have no value, but the motivation with which you make the choice is where the value lies.

You have asked to Awaken. You have asked to experience the true state of your Being. Is it not therefore absolutely congruent with all the principles that you are learning that this is what you will receive? And as we speak of manifesting a support system for the physical experience, do so in a way that is equally congruent with your realization of your Being. Therein lies the value of your recognizing the parallel aspects of manifesting within the physical experience and extending your creative nature in the state of Reality. The recognition that it is a parallel course, albeit confined to the physical experience, is the important issue. How could you dream to make something to support the physical experience while believing that the creation of it was necessary to support your real Being? And that's what happens when you place importance on the thing you manifest as opposed to the process of the manifesting.

Simply allow things to come into your awareness. Allowing is the expression of your natural Being. You will recognize the ego taking part in the process when you recognize the urge to accomplish.

In the past when you have attempted to manifest things from the standpoint or basis of fear or a need or sense of lack, these things have not been manifest. I suggest to you that the fact that they have not is congruent with your request of Awakening. If they had been manifested when you had attempted to bring them into existence from the basis of fear, they would not be confirming of the true identity of your Being. You have not asked to be further fooled. Your request has been to remember the true nature of your Self. Therefore, is it not more simply understood that everything that happens to you happens to you in absolutely perfect congruence with this request? And when your ego requests something that does not appear, you will know that your request has been granted again.

Once we understand that, then is this physical experience like a playground?

The kind of playground you are referencing is not confined to physical experience. It exists in whatever state or dimension you happen to be in where you retain the sense of limitation. It could be confusing to encourage you to have a sense of playing within the dream and to concurrently encourage you to wake up from the dream. A more helpful focus for your attention is simply that it is a dream. And by a dream, I mean it is a sense of yourself that is not real. In the sense that you have made a physical backdrop as the stage upon which to perform your comedy/drama, knowing that the part you are playing is but a caricature of your Self, do think of it as a playground. And with this recognition, play your part joyfully.

I would also encourage you to know that the joy you experience relieved of the limitation of dreaming far exceeds the "fun" that you categorize yourself as having while playing within the dream.

Experiencing Your Thoughts

One of our principal questions relates to the way in which we are conducting ourselves and the status of our financial affairs. We've been, to the best of our ability, following guidance in our activities and resisting effort, choosing to do those things which give us peace. Everything is going well except it is getting exceedingly hard for us to make ends meet financially. Are we doing the right thing or should we shift our attention to some other activities which would make it easier for us to get by each month?

There are two areas to which I would direct your attention in regard to this question. The first deals with your concern as to what you are interpreting as following the guidelines that you are learning about bringing money into your area of perceived need. What I would like to say to you is that there is too much emphasis being placed on the specific form. This seems to be a tendency that arises as one studies the philosophies that are perceived as being a path toward enlightenment. I would like you to understand that there are no formal intricacies involved in this path. Think of it more clearly as your trying to put yourself in a peaceful state of mind that remembers that which already is. And for this, I am sure you can readily understand, there is no formula.

The belief has become too cemented in your mind that there is something that you need to do to change who you are, as opposed to just allowing yourself to recognize what already Is. When you believe that there is something that you need to learn in order to, for example, manifest an adequate income, that perception, I will tell you, is backwards. Direct your attention again to what we have said many times before: there is only one thing going on and that is the process of the recognition of your Self. That process is best recognized by adjusting your simple day to day thought patterns to be more in alignment with who you Are.

Let me say it this way: a peaceful, loving, unconditionally allowing attitude brings to your conscious mind a closer alignment of the recognition of your whole Mind. If it were this process only that you were concerned with, you would find all of the other things that you perceive to be necessary to maintain your physical life would be met, and they would be met in a most natural way without a sense of effort, without any sense at all that there was something that needed to be changed other than your pattern of thinking.

You see, when you are in alignment with your natural state of peace and harmony and being the extension of Love that you truly Are, that state of Mind knows quite securely what is necessary to provide for your physical comforts. The assurance that goes along with this state of Mind brings clarity, and then that clarity is translated beautifully into what you would determine as meeting your needs.

What is currently happening is a state of confusion, and a state of confusion must, of necessity, leave your mind in doubt. The doubts are interpreted by your ego as a fear that you are not doing the right thing to manifest your needs. And in that lack of clarity and doubt, what you are perceiving as a need to be fulfilled will not happen.

The second area to address would be this: You are at all times totally, fully and completely experiencing the embodiment of your thought system. I would go further and tell you that at each and every moment you are the embodiment of that thought system. So now you see, if you couple the first with the second, it will be more easily understood that when that thought system becomes one of knowing and trust, the extension more truly of who you really Are, then that will be the embodiment of what you experience. I would encourage you not to direct your attentions towards what you may perceive as specific avenues of manifestation or other tangents, but to concentrate more basically on knowing who you Are.

Let me refresh your memory as to some of the things that you are not: You are not confusion, you are not anger, you are not fear. But when these things, these thoughts or feelings are in your conscious mind then they will, in fact, be experienced. Please do not understand or interpret this as being a negative thing or another reason to judge yourself as being lacking. More clearly understand that all things that come to you are coming to you in direct response to what you have requested. You have requested them by allowing them to be in your mind.

So I say again, there is nothing to change but your mind. It will be most helpful for you to remember that this change is not one that results in an effort on your part to do something or think something that is other than that which already exists in your Mind. What already exists there is being covered up by an illusion of who you think you are. So don't undertake this process of changing your mind with an attitude that says, "I must become something." Approach it more directly with a secure knowing on your part that the change is merely bringing you back into a realignment with what you have always been. Think of it, if you will, as a process of bringing yourself out of a state of amnesia.

Does this mean then that we will not experience prosperity and abundance in our lives until we have reached a point of living without confusion, anger, disharmony in any way? Somehow I have a hard time believing that we have to be perfect before we can start experiencing our abundance.

You misunderstood. My intent was to convey to you that what is necessary is to be perfectly clear. You see, to make the statement that says, "We need to be perfect in order to experience abundance," is again putting the equation upside down. You are already perfect. There is no need for you to strive for perfection. You need more simply to recognize that which you already Are. The fact that you are not already experiencing abundance simply indicates that you are not allowing yourself to be in a position to receive it, and that is happening because your mind exists in a state of confusion. The emphasis, if you will, has been placed upon the effect instead of the cause.

You are undoubtedly aware of and can point out many examples of people who experience great financial wealth and who are not at all, in terms that you would describe, spiritually aware. I will assure you, however, that in the cases that you would mention, there is great clarity in the mind of that individual as to what it is they wish to experience. And I would say to you this moment, that should you choose to experience financial abundance and this becomes the sole emphasis that you hold in your mind to the exclusion of all other interests, then you will have it, not because it has been bestowed upon you as a gift, but more simply, because it is held in your mind with total clarity.

Now you are asking how that fits with what I have described before as allowing a peaceful state of mind to manifest the same thing. Both have arrived because of the clarity that exists, but one has come about because that has been the sole intent of what is to be achieved, and the other occurs as a natural result of your quest for a state of peace which is the recognition of the process taking place as an answer to your total question, "Who am I?" What happens in your physical experience in the light of being in this frame of mind, is the experience of seeing yourself as whole. The experience of achieving financial wealth, when that has been the sole focus, will be perceived by you as simply having money.

So you see, in either case, both are the embodiments of your state of mind. In each case, you will recognize that which you have received. When you request, focus and direct your clear, undivided attention on wealth, you will recognize that is what you receive. When you direct your sole, undivided and clear attention on understanding who you are, then you will recognize that this is what you receive, and the financial abundance that you will experience as a result will be further recognized by you as only having the importance that it truly has. You will then see it as simply a by-product, as opposed to the beginning and the end of everything that you are seeking.

You have heard but you have not believed what I have said in regard to your absolute ability to bring into your awareness within the physical embodiment anything that you hold in your mind with total clarity. This to you has no basis that you can rely upon from your past experience and therefore, you seemingly have no reason to put faith into it. When I encourage you to ignore all other diversions except the search for the memory of who you Are, I do so with the firm knowledge that once you have grasped the significance and the knowing that comes from this, you will no longer feel a need for justification of any nature from those things you have previously experienced. The trust and the faith of the process that simply emanates from this knowledge will then become secure within you, and there will be no lack of clarity as to what is in your mind and what you are directly experiencing as a result of its being there.

You see, all of the things that appear to be hurdles can only be answered by the knowledge that comes from this quest. It is only the ego that keeps you firmly locked into putting trust and faith in those things which you have previously experienced. And so it constantly becomes the challenge, if you will, of allowing yourself to drift beyond the ego's barrier. You will not recognize yourself or the truth of what I am suggesting as long as you accept the ego's interpretation of "show me."

I think it would be appropriate here to make the circle complete and draw your attention to the first thing we spoke about in our conversation. Do not become overly concerned or misdirected by anything that you would interpret as a program or a process to accomplish that of which we have been speaking. All roads that you are taking lead surely to the answer of your primary question of, "Who am I?"

What I am suggesting to you is that you take the limited-access highway, which has fewer exits and allows for less diversion of your thinking. Allow the simplicity of living your life to be congruent and consistent with the expression of your Self, the expression and the embodiment of the Love that your Father created you to Be. It is within this loving framework that you know peace. Therefore, seek for peace to understand the Love. This is not a hypothetical or intellectual way to approach the issue . . . it is the only way for you to understand and recognize the response to your original question, which was, "Who am I?"

There are no other questions and there truly are no other answers that are fitting to be perceived by you. All other things will be diversionary and will indeed inhibit your total understanding. Learning how to manifest wealth would teach you nothing; understanding that all things flow to you as an extension of your Being is to understand everything. So, please do not confuse the issues or think that one is predicated upon the other. Understand clearly, there is but one question and one answer.

The Gifts of God

The Course talks about the gifts of God meeting all of our needs. I used to think that those were meeting the needs of form, but am I now correct in realizing that those gifts of God are not physical?

The gifts of God truly are not physical. The gift of God is you and all that you Are, the scope of you that is the scope of Him. Now, that gift having been given to you, what you do with it brings to you all of the other things which you would categorize in this physical state as being "gifts." I would suggest that once you have seen yourself beyond the limitations you now impose, you would not categorize these things as being gifts at all. They would simply be accompaniments; things that were attached to the experience you have chosen to have. All things of physical or material form are manifested as an accommodation to illustrate the experiences you have chosen.

Are they aspects of our entire Self as God created us that we have allowed ourselves to recognize and accept?

Let me say to you that basically, the You that God created exists solely and fully in the form of Love. Now, what you decide to do with the power of that Love constitutes the choosing of an experience. And when that experience puts you in a state of mind that allows you to believe that you are separate from God, that you are less than what God created, then you develop a sense of need. You will then begin to search for something to fill that need. Being unaware of your own abilities to fulfill whatever need you have, you will look outside yourself and ask for a gift. And in the asking, you acknowledge the limitation of who you think you are.

There is nothing that exists, within or around any experience you may choose to have, that is not totally and constantly present within the scope of that experience. The dichotomy would appear to be that you may choose an experience which you consciously feel would be most desirous to you, that of enjoying a happy, fun-filled life, yet it would appear to take more financial resources to fulfill that experience than you have at your disposal. What I would encourage you to understand is that the financial limitations exist because you do not accept that money flows to you as freely as your belief allows it to happen.

Everything to fulfill your experience is present when you have no limitations on receiving it. It is only when you are in a state of feeling there is need or lack, and you are not paying attention to the reality of the experience but seeing only a portion of it, that you feel there is a need to make something else to fulfill that experience. And at that point, you become quite interested in the process called manifestation.

Feeling a need to manifest occurs as you see yourself wanting something that your rational mind tells you is beyond your logical ability to have. It is most often seen as invoking some mysterious cosmic law or as a gift of God as evidence of His Love. Manifesting form of any nature does not occur as the result of an "abundant universe". It takes place because you now experience yourself as being in a physical universe whose only basis for having physical form is the meaning you attach to it. Therefore, as a need arises in your mind, in order for it to become part of your physical experience, you translate its meaning into form.

You are in a perpetual state of manifesting. You are just not aware of it. You only see it happening as you focus your intent upon it. So as you feel the need to change, embellish or broaden the scope of an experience, the only thing I encourage you to understand is that there should be a concurrent recognition that all of the accouterments that are needed to bring about a change in that experience will be instantly present as soon as you have identified the parameters and released all limitations to its manifestation.

The Human Condition

The choice of experiencing what is referred to as the "human condition" is a process of experiencing limitation. There is no judgment placed upon this observation. Limitation is simply a function of what the human experience entails. I would ask you to understand at the same time that the human condition is not one that is fixed in its parameters; that is to say, it is one in which you can expand your scope of the experience of limitation. It is not possible to experience total limitlessness while in the human condition. However, it is certainly not only possible but easily grasped that you can step beyond all limitation within the human condition that would make you believe that you are at the mercy of anything outside your conscious control of things that seem to be happening to you within that condition.

It seems that most people go through life reacting to random circumstances without understanding what you are saying. If I understand you correctly, as we choose to define the kind of experience we want, we then make our own reality within this physical life and we have the power totally to decide exactly what we want to encounter and how we want to experience it.

That is correct, and the process of clearly defining the experience is the key element; that is, to have a full and complete understanding of what the experience is that you happen to be immersed in at the moment.

Why is that important?

Because without this understanding you do place yourself in a reactive state and, by its very nature, reaction presumes that something unplanned, uncalled for, has taken place. By contrast, when you are in a state of recognition as to what the experience entails, you will find it far easier to allow yourself to be secure in the knowledge that all of the accouterments are equally within your control. It is the process of recognition of what is happening that allows you to expand your attention and your awareness to encompass the totality of it, and that is what puts you beyond the stage of being a reactor.

It is not easy for people who are immersed in the feeling of being victimized to expand their vision beyond a state of being fearful of that which they are currently reacting to, and to step into a broader space to see a broader picture.

Now, let us speak for a moment about how you come into a more conscious recognition of what a total experience actually is. I call your attention to the fact that patterns could be referred to as an index to your experience when you are trying to see the whole of it, because those patterns will indicate to you more clearly what the experience is that you are involved in. They will show you what you have been experiencing. It will be through your allowing yourself to look at those patterns that you will see a range of things that have been happening in your experience. By allowing yourself to objectively view these patterns, it will become more apparent to you what it is that you have been attempting to teach yourself. As this awareness becomes more apparent, and as you look back and see how perfectly these patterns have fulfilled themselves, it will be easier for you to see that all of the pieces that were necessary for you to experience that pattern were in place. The reason I refer to it as a pattern is that it is repetitive, and the reason that it is repetitive is that there was no conscious recognition of what it was that you had determined to learn. Once you have consciously recognized the lesson, and have seen the fullness and the value that you had determined to bring to yourself through this lesson, the pattern will be ended. Its purpose will have been achieved. This is why I say to you it is most valuable to be consciously aware of what the experience you are involved in at this moment is attempting to bring to your attention.

There must be more to finishing a pattern than just seeing a pattern.

There is far more than just seeing the pattern. Finishing it requires the experience of the lesson which you have brought into your conscious awareness. It is the experience of your having lived it, so to speak, that will determine what the value of it has been. Many times you will see the value has been to show you the valuelessness of fear. But you will not experience the fact that fear has no value as long as you are in a state of simply reacting to fear. Then that thing which you have feared, in one form or another, will keep reappearing and that is what makes a pattern.

Is that also what some call "Karma?"

Karma, I would like to say, is merely an excuse for continuing a pattern that you have become comfortable with. Most often that pattern is one that says that there is good and bad, and that to experience the fullness of anything you must have experienced both aspects of it. This is only a choice. But if this is your choice, then that will be your pattern.

Judging Yourself

The Course says, "Dream of your brother's kindnesses, instead of dwelling in your dreams on his mistakes. Select his thoughtfulness to dream about instead of counting up the hurts he gave." (T-585) What am I to do when I can't seem to see the kindness and thoughtfulness?

At any moment you have an awareness that you are unable to see love in any form in someone else, know with a certainty that you are withholding that love from yourself. As you allow your awareness to increase and encompass those around you, then you will find how much more aware they appear to have become. Because, you see, nothing has changed in them; it has only been your awareness of yourself that has become open. The same is true for any emotion or feeling that you would seek to derive from a brother. It is simply a matter of allowing yourself to be open to that feeling as you see it coming from yourself.

You are looking in all of the wrong places. As you attempt to focus on an answer to a problem that you perceive as being your own, and you look for the answer as you see it expressed through another person, you are confusing the effects with the cause. *Nothing is happening for you that is not created directly by the thought patterns that you hold within your own mind.* All perceptions pertaining to the world outside your mind are made directly by those thought patterns. The world is seen through the filters of that perception, which you may or may not be consciously aware of.

Let me explain it like this: as you have developed a need to be loved, a need to see love being expressed to you, you will focus upon those outside you to bring that confirmation to your attention. You will never find it there. What you will find there is the reflection of the confusion that is in your own mind. You will see some people who will apparently reflect to you the love that you seek; you will see others reflect to you less than the love that you seek. This is the confusion that lies within your own mind. You must understand quite clearly that nothing comes to you except what comes *through* you.

What comes through you as a loving feeling is what you will find expressed in the loving feelings reflected around you. Therefore, you must concentrate only on why it is that you do not feel these loving feelings as being a part of you, as being something that comes through you, as being an extension of you.

I will remind you of something: you are at this moment nothing less than complete and total Love. Instead of hearing this as simply being a message of words, allow it to go deeper. You must allow it to bypass your intellectual understanding. You must stop being afraid of understanding that there is nothing about the real you that is not constituted solely of Love. I am not offering you encouragement—I am simply stating a fact to you. As the perfect creation of the Father, it is impossible for you to be less than what I have described. For you to be less than that would make Him less than that.

Once you have allowed yourself even the beginning of this understanding, you will find the world around you beginning to change dramatically. Feel good about that change, but do not let it be mysterious. Understand that it is changing because you are changing the way you see yourself. That is the only way for your world outside, as you see it, to change.

The world around you is simply a place that waits for your manifestations to be cast upon it. As you cast fear upon it, cast doubt upon it, then that will be your experience of it. But if you allow the experience of Love to be developed within you, it will also reflect to you the experience of Love.

It would be much easier if all you had to do was wait to see the love that came to you from others. Then it would require nothing on your part. But if this were true, then you would remain forever a victim of the world. I will tell you that the physical, outside dimension of the world as you now see it is nothing but a prisoner of your thinking.

Do not judge yourself for being less a person when you are unable to see a positive response to you from many of those around you, or when you are unable to see the Love that you have been told exists within those people around you. You are simply setting up more excuses to be judgmental about yourself, and this will only perpetuate the pattern that I have spoken to you about. It is now time to change the pattern. And for you, my brother, that pattern can only be changed by giving up the misperceptions of who you are. I am not asking you to become something that you are not. I am not really asking you to change anything. I am simply asking you to let go of your *misperception.*

As you now find it extremely difficult not to be judgmental about other people, understand that this is so because you cannot avoid judging yourself. I ask you to go within and ask yourself if it is your belief that you are being judged by God. And when you have satisfied yourself that you are not, then ask yourself, "If God judges me not, then why do I persist in this activity? If God sees me as being His loving Son, then why do I withhold that feeling from myself?"

Old patterns are hard to discard. Your intellect and your ego will give you many things to do to change these patterns. There will appear to be many books, many wise teachers, all of whom will help you, but in the final analysis it will be only you who will seek out the quiet time to allow this feeling of God's Love to totally immerse you, to always be with you. Allow yourself to respond to that Love by allowing yourself whatever moments of joy you can each day. You will be surprised at the small things that will bring you joy if you but allow yourself to be worthy of accepting them. There will be no apparent external reasons that will come to you, no logic that will present itself as saying, "This I am entitled to." This is the feeling that must come from within you. This is the basic decision that you must make to simply be happy.

I know that it is your desire to please God, and I would have you know there is no greater way for you to do this than to be joyful. It is totally unimportant what you are joyful about—it is simply the choice of allowing yourself to be in a state of joy.

Chapter Four

Differences and Truth

"Where you are in this process of loving determines your ability to understand truth."

Appreciating Differences And Experiencing Truth

The issue I would like to clarify for you at this time is the one that exists in your perception regarding why it appears that all people who are seeking to understand who they are do not seem to understand, or gravitate toward, what you consider to be the most appropriate message. What you are seeking to understand is a universal truth that can be perceived in a single fashion; a single message, as it were. The truth that you are losing sight of is the fact that all of you—and I am using the term "all" to be totally encompassing—who still see yourselves as being asleep are not really asleep. You are Awake at this moment. The totality of your Being is well aware of who it Is. To convince the limited aspect you have made and identified yourself as being—which I call the ego—that it is, in fact, Awake will be arrived at through whatever means the ego allows.

This may sound strange to you, but because you have identified yourself as being an ego, then it must be through the ego that the message will arrive that you are not an ego. And in as much as there are as many perceived reasons for believing you are asleep as there are egos that appear to be sleeping, then the message as it is allowed to be perceived will be different. And it should not concern you that each will only allow that message which he is capable of hearing at that moment to reach him.

I have mentioned to you many times before that there is but one thing for you to be concerned about and that is your own Awakening. Please allow me to assure you that as this unfolds, you will realize quite clearly that it is in your Awakening process that the message you are currently attempting to convey will be, shall I say, automatically understood by any other who is seeking to accomplish the same thing. I will also assure you that he or she may not perceive it or see it as being arrived at in the same fashion, on the same path that you have chosen. They will simply see who they are through your Vision of yourself, and they will instinctively know the correct route for them to take to clarify their own Vision.

We have spoken of the little word called "motivation". When it is in your heart to extend your Being, no matter how you may perceive it at that particular moment, that becomes an acceptance of who you are, and in the sharing of it, you demonstrate that recognition to yourself. If there is an expectation that it will be received as having some significant effect on the recipient, then your motive has become non-illustrative to the point I have described. Also know that it is not important for you to focus on being an example, because that carries with it the implication that you are expecting others to see what you are and thereby changes your own focus as to the importance of what is really happening.

I do have such a sense of satisfaction in sharing your truth with others because I know it has been so changed in the Bible. Are you saying that this is not really important?

Were you to see this from my and your undistorted point of view, you would see that you are already perfectly expressed. There is nothing about you that is lacking. There is nothing about you that does not perfectly express the Love of our Father. What I also see is that you are sleeping. In your state of current conscious awareness, when you see any brother in his sleep, would you criticize him for being asleep and tell him that his dreams are not as good as yours? Or will you rest in the total assurance that when he is ready he will wake up?

Yet I know that our process of waking up is sometimes aided by information that comes to us from different sources. It feels to me that the transcription of these dialogues could serve this function for someone.

Indeed, there will be many who will be served by such information. They will be served by it as they allow themselves to come to a recognition, a point of view you might say, that allows them to hear what I am telling you. It will be most helpful for you to understand at the same time that there are many others who do not share this point of view and I will speak to them differently. I will speak to them in the language that is best heard by them.

Please remember what I said earlier. The truth is that you have never changed your Being. The illusion is that there is only one way for you to understand that you are already Awake. You are attempting to reconcile what I have given you as Truth to a single point of view of understanding that Truth. And what I am attempting to explain to you is that the full impact, the full awareness and knowledge of that Truth, will not be fully known by you until you recognize yourself as being It. So do attempt to allow your perception of it to be unlimited. Simply recognize this truth: you will experience the totality of your Self, and all others will share in the experience from the point of view to which they are best able to accommodate their ego understanding.

I tell you that I am with you always. I will tell you that it is impossible for me not to be with you always because we are One. And it is that Oneness that I am encouraging you to now let develop as a thought form. It is to merge the identification that you have ascribed to me as being the identification of you. We are truly, in the only meaningful way, brother/sister; an equally expressed, perfect extension, indistinguishably the same extension of our Father. No more was given to me than was given to you. It was appropriate for a while for me to encourage you to dwell on the feelings that you have for me. It would be totally inappropriate for me at this time not to begin to encourage you to recognize those feelings as being applicable to yourself. Indeed, I am telling you that if given to me but withheld from you, they lose their meaning.

Are you saying that the special love I feel for you is something I should recognize as being my capability of expressing that love to others since it comes from our common Source?

Sit for a moment and allow yourself to recognize the reasons that you designate me as being so worthy of this wonderful love that you give. What am I in your definition that makes me worthy of such feeling?

Because I see you as being totally Awake.

But you see, I see you as being Awake. And it is my encouragement to you to realize that there is not one reason that you could conjure up for having this feeling about me that is not equally true about you. You only think you are asleep. You are only coming from a point of view that allows you to see yourself as being asleep. So see through my eyes. See yourself as I see you. See yourself with the Vision of the Christ and concurrently recognize that it is your Vision. That is the beauty of it all. It is easy for you to translate the Vision of the Christ as being my Vision, because it is easy for you to see me being the Christ. So accept that. Accept my Vision and allow me to share with you that I see through your eyes.

There is no Vision I possess that is exclusive of your Vision.

The Recognition of Truth

I was reading in The Urantia Book *that you explained to the disciples that although the personalities of men varied, all Sons of God at the level of the Self have the same recognition of Truth because we are all from the same Source. I think I had interpreted this as all men should then understand the same words as truth, which you have just explained is not so. Did you then mean . . .*

No, allow me to interrupt. Each Self recognizes the same Truth because the expression of Truth is who you are. But as long as you view yourself as being different from who you really are, as long as your thinking is an illusion of Truth, then those things that will trigger the recognition of your Self and Truth will appear to vary dramatically. The underlying Truth will not change. The essence of your Being does not change. It is only while you are in a frame of mind that is illusory of right thinking that the reasons and ways to correct that right thinking will appear to come in different ways. The words that will trigger your recognition of your Self, your recognition of truth, will be different than the words which will trigger the exact same recognition in someone else. The Truth doesn't change; only the vehicle which is necessary to accomplish your recognition of it will change.

Would it be correct to say that as one expresses the Truth of who he is, a Love is being expressed that is recognized by all because it is touching the sameness within us all of the expression of God?

How beautifully expressed! Now, couple this with the understanding that as that recognition dawns upon whomever chooses to see it, the words that form in the mind of that person, the concepts which trigger that recognition, may be totally different than what triggered you to the same recognition. But you have both arrived at the same point of recognition because that is the only point that does, in reality, exist.

Is there anything that is true for all time or do we enter into different perception levels of Truth?

In its purest sense, the word "Truth" would be completely interchangeable with the word Creator, or God, or Love, and in that context, it would be eternal. It would not be finite. When you ask is truth fixed, you must then ask yourself the question is Creation fixed. And I will tell you it is not. It is an ever changing affair, but its meaning is absolutely unchanging in that it describes a feeling of absolutely accepting Love.

Where you are within this process of Loving determines your ability to understand truth. While you see yourself dancing around the periphery of Love and experiencing more of the emotional aspects of it, then your definition of truth will be very perceptual and it will appear to change as your understanding changes. But when you allow yourself to become more deeply enmeshed, giving up more of the limitations to understanding Love and simply become the act of extending Love, then you have given up more of the limiting conditions under which you are willing to give Love and your perception becomes one of knowing the meaning of Truth.

There have been many attempts to describe an energy force out of which the universe is constructed. This energy force is one that can only be described as Love. As you take this force and mix it in your coloring pots and with your brushes, apply it to the canvas that you imagine life and the universe to be, you will see the perception of truth take many shapes and forms. And in that light, you will begin to wonder how definite truth can be because you perceive yourself molding it and changing it to suit your instantaneous need. My encouragement to you is to see the paint in the pot as being the absolute, not the way it is applied to the canvas but in its essential form as it resides in wholeness within your coloring pot. Identify yourself with the paint as it exists before it is perceptually applied to the canvas, and you will know the meaning of Truth.

Any attempt that is made to put a description on the Essence of Creation must, of necessity, establish boundaries that do not exist around it. It is only the intellect that needs to understand something by packaging it. Let go of the need! Recognize that you *are* Truth. You are the paint in the pot and it is your mind and your perceptions that cause you to believe that you can spread it on the canvas and make something different of it. Allow yourself to *be* spread, so to speak, by seeing your Self as being the flow of Creation, which is the paint that has already been applied to the canvas by your Creator. And as you experience yourself as being that, you will know that whatever you express in that context is the expression of Truth and it is you. You can no more be separate from Truth than you can be separate from God.

There is no difference between the definitions you are attempting to achieve as you would define God, Love, Truth or Creation. This thing that has been referred to as "illusion" is only a perception that there is a difference between those things and that you are not an integral part of It.

Instead of searching for a definition of Truth, search for a definition of your Self to clear the confusion in your mind that exists between knowing who you are and the pretending who you are not. It can only be through your allowing these misperceptions to melt away that you will experience yourself as the flow of the Creator's brush *with no willful effort on your part to determine the scene that is being painted.* You are the paint. You are the brush. But the creation of the canvas has already been done. Allow yourself the joy of recognizing the perfection with which it has been done and you will know the definition of Love.

Communication

Can you speak about communication with discarnate beings?

As you become more familiar with being in contact with your whole Mind, you will soon understand that which you call "communication with discarnate beings" is a very natural and perpetual occurrence. Those things that you now think of as being extraordinary are really quite ordinary as you remove the barriers to experiencing more of your Self. You will begin to develop the sense that there isn't really such a gap between those who are in body and those who are not. As thoughts that you have are responded to in a form of communication that is as clear to you as a verbal dialogue with a friend three feet away, you begin to understand experientially that the Essence of you is not identifiable as a body. It soon becomes obvious that because you are communing mind to mind there is no "space" between those minds that is not bridged by a single change of focus in your attention. And this becomes a foundation for remembering that when you have again accepted the wholeness of your Mind, you will not experience it as being separate from any other mind. The familiarity of feeling of unified Mind begins to register with you.

You will also discover, as you experience the harmony within this unity, that there is no feeling of a distinction made between that which is being expressed and experienced by one and that which is acknowledged as the expression and experience of any other.

It is only when you accept that which you call a "personality" that you develop the fear that your personality lacks something, and in the lacking, you need to shield yourself from the recognition of those around you. When you remember that there is nothing to be shielded from, when you recognize the joy that exists in the sharing of the experience as being the extension of unity, then you will understand why there are no barriers between communications as they exist within the Father's Creation.

Does that include plant or animal life?

I would not exclude any expression of Creation. You find this difficult to accept because of the perception you have made about these other expressions. As you see them having a form which presents a barrier to your acknowledged ability to communicate, you then presume that no communication is possible. When you allow yourself to experience everything that exists as being the expression of Creation in its pure form as a single life force, then you acknowledge the purity of your form and will recognize the ability of these forms to communicate. I use the word "communicate" in a broader sense than you are accustomed to experiencing. Speaking, the flow of words, is a very minuscule attempt to communicate. It will be on the level of feeling, and only on that level, that you will experience and understand my meaning.

Am I correct in my thinking that there is no difference in the essence of life between this cat sitting by me and myself because we are both the energy or the creation of God?

That is correct.

Mankind has thought itself to be a superior being to the animals and plants. Is that a misperception ?

To understand the basis for this question, allow yourself to remember this: you will experience only that which is a result of the process of your thinking. You have developed what I could term a caricature of yourself, and to that caricature you have given all of the attributes that are commonly accepted as the human condition.

One of those attributes is that the human condition is superior. And because of that feeling of superiority, your perceptions of other things within Creation have been misconstrued, which is to say, you do not see them in their truest Light. You see them in the light that allows them to fit within the categories that you have allowed to be acceptable. I will say to you again: all things within Creation exist at a level of perfection. There is no hierarchy that is expressed within perfection. Your perception now allows you to see only that which is acceptable to the thought patterns which you have adopted.

Where did the statement in the Bible come from that man had been given dominion over all things? Was that a mistake or not accurate?

That is, in fact, a misperception. The meaning that was attempted to be communicated was that man had dominion *over his own thoughts* and so also over what those thoughts made manifest. And within that realm, he would in no way be a victim to any circumstances that he subsequently did experience.

That's a major misunderstanding. I imagine that there must be many others.

Within the illusion there are many misunderstandings. I would not encourage you to direct your attention to the discovery of these, but more appropriately to the discovery of how you can rise above experiencing limitation, of denying your Divinity. Becoming aware of who you Are, and bringing that awareness into your experiences within the physical body is a beautiful challenge. That awareness can enhance, completely beyond your current understanding, the experience in a physical body.

If we keep seeking, will the barriers simply remove themselves to this greater awareness?

Your desire forms the foundation for this happening. It is this desire, which I would call a decision, that is the key element in that which you term "seeking." It will be this decision that will provide the constant encouragement for you to continue to open up your thinking to greater possibilities. What you are doing each time you simply accept the notion that there is something more to be experienced is creating a little void, a little niche within that thought system that allows new information to be experienced.

That which you are is omnipresent; that which you think you are is fragmented or isolated. Each new idea that opens your mind heals the sense of isolation, expanding your willingness to more clearly see that which is present. I remind you that when you use the term "seeking" it is well to remember that you already have it, and what you are attempting to do is to remove whatever veils currently cover it up.

Is part of our process of remembering the process of channeling like Tom is doing, or is that only one aspect of many choices?

I would have to say that this is as variable as any other choice made by one who has chosen to wake up. It may serve a purpose that is more immediately apparent, and it may not. It should not be seen in any way as being the only avenue, or even a special avenue. Please understand that once you have made the commitment to yourself to remember who you Are, all avenues which you allow yourself to be directed onto will be those that will bring to you the most perfect expression of an answer to your quest. So-called "channeling", if seen as a message from a Being greater than or disconnected from you is not particularly helpful.

In the truer sense, if the experience of channeling is accepted as an acknowledgment of the removal of a barrier which you have believed to exist between the limited version of yourself and the unlimited reality of your Self, it is very helpful. It illustrates that, indeed, there was no barrier to begin with. Any acknowledgment made by you, whether it is through the direct or indirect experience of what we are calling "channeling" as simply being the removal of another sense of being separate from your brothers or your Father, is very valuable.

In the process of listening to my own inner voice, I sometimes get two voices and sometimes they're conflicting as to what they say. What kind of process could I use to get beyond this confusion?

Which voice brings you peace? Whichever voice that is at that moment, then please listen to it. Do not concern yourself with the feeling of needing to be in the Presence of absolute Truth. Concern yourself more with the desire to be at peace. It will be the building of this habit that will merge the voices into one.

There is much importance and emphasis placed on being able to discern between voices. Whether you recognize them as originating from yourself, or from a source outside of you, there is no difference. This desire, this determination, to recognize which voice speaks Truth seems to resonate with you as being important because you believe that it will be in your recognition of Truth that you are able to confirm that you are in the process of Awakening.

Recognize that the process of Awakening is the making of the ego. Please allow me to say that again as it bears great relevance. *The process of Awakening is a concept of the ego. You are Awake. You are completely whole.* You do not see it. Therefore, it seems apparent to you that there is a process involved in allowing yourself to overcome it, and that is the game of your ego. There is nothing to overcome . . . there is only to let go of your illusion.

It is the letting go process that is facilitated by being in a peaceful state. How many times have you recognized yourself as being in a peaceful state and concurrently recognized that there was something for you to do? Have you ever thought about that? If your natural state is one of being at peace, then why, when you are not at peace, does it seem so rationally logical that you are on the right path to waking up by doing all the things you have convinced yourself it is necessary to do in order to wake up?

Please, just be at peace. Whichever voice speaks to you at the moment, in words or feelings or thoughts that put you in feelings of peace, be with that voice. What it is telling you to do is absolutely unimportant. *The feeling with which you respond to the words is the only thing which should be of value to you.* It will never be the doing that will bear any relevance to your waking up. It will only be the accompanying feeling, and when that feeling is one of peace, then you are in harmony with the moment, with the need of that very moment. So please, don't worry about what it was telling you to do, just how you felt about it. Don't focus so much on what you do, but more on why you do it.

I have been told that beings on the other side of the threshold cannot openly communicate with the earth plane, and that it requires someone who loves them very much to open that communication from this side.

As I have referred your attention to the basis of communication being the feelings of Love, do you not understand that as you carry those feelings of Love with you today for another who has left physical form the bond of communication is in place?

Do you mean verbally?

No. I will tell you that this is the reason I have attempted to redirect your thinking as to what communication really is. Communication on the level of Loving takes place through the message and the *feeling* of Love, and as you hold those feelings, you share it even now.

Your desire to strike up a conversation on a verbal level is more to answer an intellectual need and curiosity which you currently have. I encourage you to understand that curiosity of this form does not enhance the path upon which you have set yourself. Letting go of your intellectual curiosity and allowing yourself to relax into the trust of your feelings of Love are what will eventually allow you to communicate on the truest level possible throughout the universe, wherever you direct your attention with that Loving feeling.

Did you know me when you walked the earth?

There has never been a time when I have not known you. There has never been a time when *you* have not known every expression of God. You know deep within you that the feeling of limited acquaintances that appears to be so finite within the human experience is simply an illusion, a case of not being able to remember. As you represent the fullest expression of what God Is, and you know that every other one represents the same, how would it be possible for infinite knowing not to know the whole?

I am asking you to step beyond this wall of seeing your experiences as having only had value as you can catch glimpses of your memory of prior times. This can be a severe limitation. It is a focus that shackles your attention to a very narrow framework of experience. I am encouraging you to allow this to pass. As I reinforce to you that you hold the knowledge of all Creation, I suggest that you remove the barriers to your thinking that prevents you from experiencing this fullness.

Information About Jesus

Is The Aquarian Gospel accurate in the depiction of your life 2,000 years ago, and are other sources such as The Gnostic Gospels, Lessons from the Aquarian Age, and The Urantia Book also accurate?

There are aspects of truth and there are aspects of perception of truth. It will be more helpful if you begin to divorce the connection you have made between my word and the words of Truth that you are fully capable of recognizing at any moment that you choose.

I cannot specifically answer your question because you are calling for a general conclusion which cannot be made. As I have stated, there is Truth present and there is perception of truth present. Perception of truth may be distorted based upon the one who is perceiving it and the fears that he may have at any given time. I have said to you do not dwell upon the words. Try more closely to be in touch with feelings that are generated within you as words are communicated to you and evoke responses from you. *Pay attention to the feelings.* Words will have the tendency to separate you from their source.

Our path is one that attempts to heal separation. Let us not dwell upon any aspect of truth or perception as it may be communicated in any way that seems to foster judgments and results in feelings of separation. *Love your brother no matter what he says.* Honor the feelings of Love that are within you which reach out and embrace and recognize the feelings of Love that are within him and which go beyond the very narrow boundaries and limitations that communication through words presents.

Should there be one who loved me dearly and then, because of subsequent fears, wrote of his perceptions of me and my teachings using a filter through which his perceptions caused his words to flow in a way that made them less meaningful to you, would that destroy the Love that was the essence of the message? The whole point of everything I try to communicate would be destroyed were you to believe that this were possible. *Words are tools of the intellect. Feelings are expressions of your Spirit.* Allow the words to communicate as clearly as possible the feelings of Love you would have them do, but please do not be bound or separated because the words would have a different meaning to those to whom they were offered. When you stand in their presence, extending the Love of your Being with no words being necessary, then miscommunication is impossible. Ask yourself how many times you have attempted to communicate and although you felt yourself to be quite clear there were, nevertheless, misunderstandings. Please hear my point: Go beyond the words. Reside in the feelings that represent who you Are and know that the recognition of you is most clearly expressed by that and that alone.

The Bible states that one should not listen to spirits and some people interpret this to mean the process of communication that we are sharing now. Could you help us to understand why that is in the Bible?

There existed during that time the belief that evil spirits could inhabit the body of one brother or another. As this brother went about in what was termed to be a state of insanity, it was believed that those who were weak of will could be influenced by this insanity. And, therefore, the custom developed to exorcise the demon or evil as it appeared to exist within the body.

I would additionally have you know that I never engaged in the process of leading a brother to believe that his or any other body was in possession of a "demon" or an "evil spirit". Then, as now, perceptions of my acts and my deeds will vary. They may, in some instances, be reflective of the true intention I had, and they may, in some instances, not be reflective of that.

Why did you choose Tom Carpenter to manifest your communication through? Did he choose you or was it simultaneous?

I would say that we chose each other. It is part of his process in learning to accept and trust who he Is. In the doing of this process in which we are currently engaged, his purpose is being fulfilled. It is the purpose which, on his path, will most suitably enhance his Awakening process.

It is not a special or miraculous treatment. It should not be seen as in any way enhancing him or what he is experiencing or what his path may be over a path that would be chosen by any other.

Do you manifest in this manner through many others at this time?

Many others, yes.

It would be appropriate here for me to give you a different understanding as to what happens when one asks for guidance. As we have discussed before, there is the Mind which expresses God that I have called "the Christ". Within this Mind of the Christ resides the Truth of God. That Truth is, in its Essence, entirely whole. Its wholeness is expressed by each unique and individual expression that resides in it. But each expression knowing itself will express this Truth in a slightly different fashion. This expression of Truth, in an infinite number of ways, is what is called the movement of Creation.

Now, as one expression of this Mind may exist in a state of not knowing that he is an expression of this Mind, that brother would not be in possession of true knowledge of himself. As he then seeks to remember himself, he does so within his belief system, or what I have called a dream state. He uses the ego's tools that are available to him within the dream. Memories of experiences he has had within this and many other dreams are available to him. As he picks one out that to him becomes representational of one of his brothers who has remembered who he is, he seizes upon this identification as being an avenue for him to regain his own memory.

I will use the specific example of myself and Tom. As he has remembered me and identified me as being what I would call his "ticket home," his attention lies on the wisdom that he perceives as being embodied within me as the expression of the Christ. Because that attention is comfortable and identifiable to him, he is able to relate to it and, therefore, chooses to separate it out from an infinite number of other expressions of truth believing that the information that comes from me is that which is embodied in who I Am.

As he becomes more aware that my individuality is of no consequence but simply a representation of the truth of the Christ, he can allow his attention to expand into his own awareness of his being an equal expression of the Christ.

So as you would ask me how many others I speak to, my answer to you most appropriately would be to divorce myself as an individual expression of the Christ and to say that the Christ, the Truth that is embodied within the Christ, is expressed through many and it is no different than the truth which I express to Tom.

I continually encourage you to look beyond the identification of any single expression of the Christ. See the Christ as being unified because it will be in your seeing its unification that you will more easily be able to accept your part in it. As you hold me out and identify me as being special, you will continue to find reasons why you are not special enough to fit into that category. Our conversations are designed to unite us within the Mind of God. Should I give you information that would exalt me and fail to encourage you to recognize yourself on an equal footing, then we could not be rejoined in our proper place within the unified Mind of God.

Are these communications to others primarily within the United States or are they throughout the world?

I would encourage you to understand that thinking in terms of "throughout the world" would be far too limiting. In all of Creation, there are expressions who know themselves and expressions who do not. And those who do will speak to those who don't at any opportunity. In the case to which you are referring, on this planet, many throughout the planet are being spoken to.

Chapter Five

The Life of Jesus

"I urge you not to focus on my process. Do not allow yourself to become buried in the thoughts that are brought to your mind by seeing me nailed to a cross. For I will tell you that you have nailed yourself to many crosses, and while they appear to be different, they are not. While the anguish that you suffer appears to be less intense than the anguish you perceive that I suffered, it is not so. It is time now for you to give up the cross, both yours and mine."

Jesus As A Brother

Your love for me could not be of the magnitude that you feel were it not for an understanding on your part that it is a whole Love that is shared between us. It is the Love that, as we see it reflected between us, is a pure acknowledgment of the Love of our Father. And it in is this sense that makes the love you feel for me appear to be special, while indeed, it is not. It is the familiarity that arises as you recognize in me Love being totally whole, because in that recognition you not only find the expression of me, but of every other one. It is not, I'm sure you are aware, a Love that simply focuses on an individual, but a Love that recognizes the wholeness of Self which is the incorporation of All That Is—of every brother and of the totality of the Mind of God. That is not to say that at this moment I do not rejoice totally in what you are expressing. I assure you that I do, and I thank you for that.

Do I understand you to be saying that this wondrous feeling that I feel for you is the feeling that will grow to encompass all of God's creations as I let go of more of my illusions?

Indeed. That is absolutely correct. You will come to recognize me for what I truly am, which is the representational feeling of the Christ, as you Are.

It seems that you, as an expression of our Creator, have a special role for this planet. You have been referred to as the "Planetary Prince" of this planet. Would you care to talk about who you really are?

I will first correct a misunderstanding about the use of the term "Planetary Prince" as it was expressed in The Urantia Book. It would be more appropriate if you thought of that term, and particularly the way that it was expressed as being me, as being more representational of the Christ; that is the feeling, the embodiment of the principles and the truth of the Christ. And as you will understand, the truth of the Christ is the truth of you as abundantly as it is the truth of me. There appeared to be only one difference at that time, and that was my being more aware of it than you.

Please do not elevate me beyond the concept you think is attainable for yourself, for that would be most inappropriate. I am me, knowing that I am me, encouraging you to recognize that we are the same. There are no favorites in the family of God; there is no one who is higher than another, no one who is more illustrious, or contains more wisdom. We are all an equal extension of the Mind of God. As you think of me as being a special person, how would it feel if we exchanged places and you could see yourself as being this very special person? That is my message to you, loved one.

What has confused me in this issue is the fact that your birth was announced before the "immaculate conception" took place. It seemed as if you were not just another human being born again into the illusion.

The message that was attempted to be conveyed here was that you are not either. To be more clearly specific, there were no circumstances or events which occurred around my life here on earth that would be in any way special or different from circumstances that would involve any other brother. They appear to be more dramatic simply to illustrate the point, but not to draw attention to the person. To certainly draw attention to the feeling of being the Christ, indeed, yes. But not to draw attention to me as a specific individual who had attained anything other than what you already are.

You see, were this to be so, your attention would be always drawn to the person and miss completely the basis of the message which was to draw your attention to the Mind of God, to the essence of you which is the Divinity of All That Is. This may not be seen when your attention rests on anyone whom you conceive to be special or separate. This is the embodiment of the principle that you continuously study which expresses the Son of God. Even the explanation that the Son of God is infinitely expressed, in some cases, draws your attention away from the aspect of unity.

I still wonder how you could have come into physical embodiment and at such a young age, become aware of who you were if you were not more advanced in some way. Were you fully Awakened before you chose to come into the physical experience at that time?

Nothing really changes in your state of mind whether you are on, as you perceive it, this side of the curtain of death or the other side. Your state of mind remains the same. You are no less enlightened now than if you would be seeing yourself in a state without body. My coming to recognize and understand who I am occurred both in and out of body. And I was simply more aware, closer to the truth of myself, as I came into that incarnation. My physical age had little to do with it.

Had you had other physical experiences on this planet?

Indeed.

Would I know of any of those historically?

Indeed, you would.

Would you care to share that information?

I do not think at this point a historical exploration would be helpful. It would draw your attention to areas which are superfluous. Again, the focus of your interest should be on me only to the extent that what you see embodied in your perception of me would be an encouragement for you to know that it is also the embodiment of you. Otherwise, we are missing the point.

Have you been in the physical embodiment since the time you were here as Jesus? Is there a Being called "Maitreya" embodied as the Christ at this time and is that you?

No, I have not been in the physical embodiment again. The personification that you have known me as being "Jesus" is not the personification of the being called "Maitreya". There is but one Son and that Son is known as the Christ. As you are the Christ and I am the Christ, "Maitreya" is the Christ.

Is this someone whom I should seek out? Is Maitreya going to present himself as a spiritual leader for this time?

A true spiritual leader will never present himself or herself to you as being a spiritual leader. For one to announce they are a leader fosters the belief they are seeking followers. There have been many examples of enlightened beings who were assigned the role of leader against their wishes and in opposition to the message they offered.

One who is aware of his Self recognizes that Self equally in you and does not encourage you to become a follower, but rather to join him as an equal. He sees your perfection, the Divinity you currently hide from yourself and knows that his Vision of you strengthens your own.

When you encounter one who has recognized and accepted himself as the Christ, I assure you, no announcement of it will be necessary.

Jesus' Awareness

In your life as Jesus, when you were not in the full awareness of being the consciousness of the Christ, when you experienced pain and suffering, did you have any kind of understanding that you might have been transmuting pain and suffering for others?

Allow us to answer this question in its truer light. You are wondering as to the source of the pain and suffering you have experienced, and you are asking if it is possible for you to either take on pain from others, or through your experience of pain, to pass it on to others. I will tell you this: It is not possible for you to transmit or take on anything other than that which is reflective of the Essence of who you are, and the Essence of who you are is what I have described as being a flow of Love. All things that seem to come to you or emanate from you that are not comprised of this Essence are those things that you have made up and chosen to experience apart from your experience of being the Christ.

The analogy I would offer you is this: If the essence of your Being were expressed by a cool lake, a stream of pure water, then all you would be able to express would be that which constituted the basis of what you were. That could be fog, or mist, or drops of water, or swirling water, or calm water, but in its essence it would all be an expression of that which comprised the basis of what you are.

It would not be possible for you to express yourself as being a twig of wood. If, however, you experienced yourself as being this pool of water and you chose to believe that you could express yourself as a twig of wood, then it would be your perception that wood was what you were expressing, but it would not alter the truth of what you are. You cannot alter that which makes up your Being. And you cannot, in truth, express other than that which constitutes the Essence of your Being.

You are absolutely free, however, to change your perception about what it is that does constitute the Essence of your Being, and in that altered perception of your Self, you have additional misperceptions about many things. Among them could be that it would be possible for you to express pain, for you to inflict pain, and for you to receive pain from another. In your state of perception and belief, these things would appear to be the state of reality. But I am attempting to convey to you now that they are, in fact, not of Reality. They are of a state of mind that is a misperception of Reality.

Let me put it in another way: all things that emanate from the Source of the Creator are unchangeable. Your choice—to either experience them as being within their natural state or to see a misperception of them—is based upon your choice to either recognize the separated sense of yourself or to be in awareness of your Self as the Christ.

When you are in the Christ awareness, you will see no aspect of yourself that is apart from its Source.

When you were in the Garden of Gethsemane and the decision was made to undergo that experience, knowing that ultimately it would lead to your crucifixion, was that a decision of the Christ, or was that a decision of Jesus?

It was very clearly a decision of the man, Jesus. The cross fulfills no purpose for the Christ. Your question, however, is more directed toward seeking an understanding as to why either the man or the Christ would take on a role which appeared to be that of a martyr.

Please understand this was not the meaning of the crucifixion. There is never justification for sacrifice, for this implies it could be necessary for one brother to do something to his detriment in order to bring benefit to another. You may rest assured this kind of thinking has no place in the Mind of God and would, therefore, not be an expression of the Christ. There is no opposite to the Love God extends to His Son, and it is never given to one and withheld from another.

As the man, Jesus, there were purposes achieved for me in choosing to allow the experience of the crucifixion. Those experiences would also fulfill a purpose which would be helpful for the understanding of my brothers. The decision both fulfilled my purpose and served as an illustration to those who truly understood the meanings of my teachings at that time of how to establish a foundation for understanding infinite Life. There was no sacrifice on my part to teach this lesson. You must know my purpose was equally fulfilled. My purpose as Jesus was to recognize myself as being the entire embodiment of the Christ. Your purpose is the same.

Had I truly been sent here as a messenger from God, that would be in direct contradiction to what I have been saying to you—that you are, in fact, the perfect expression of the Father Himself and He sees you only in the light of that perfection. How then could He send me to try to teach you that?

I chose my experience. I chose it to experience my fulfillment as being the Christ, and the way that I could have my experience most distinctly understood by me was to show it to you. Principles do not change. As I ask you to see your Divinity being mirrored in the eyes of your brother, do you think it would be different for me?

When I was brought before the council of those who were to pass final judgment upon me, many have wondered why I did not more vigorously defend myself. The essence of the charge of blasphemy being levied against me was my refusal to deny my assertion of being the Son of God. Many wonder why I then did not shake loose my bonds and bring the wrath of God to bear upon those about to condemn His "only and most beloved Son." Why did I not protect myself from this "most cruel and unjust punishment" that lay ahead?

There were, in fact, those at the time who interpreted my defenselessness as validation of the charge. They reasoned that God would never permit one who was truly His Son to be treated in such a way. There were others then, and subsequently, who believe that misfortunes experienced in their lives are God's punishment for the death of His Son.

The meaning of my life's message is lost in these beliefs.

Had I reacted in a fashion in keeping with the law of an "eye for an eye," defending myself and casting others down, my life would have become justification for the belief that the sins of man and the wrath of God are real. All those who sat that day in judgment's chamber, accusers and accused, were God's Sons—not one more holy than the next. And knowing this, I could do nothing less than abide there in a state of peace and Love. To condemn them for their thoughts seen separate from the Thoughts of God gives substance to an idea impossible to be true.

Look not to other meanings founded in the illusion of fear the world seems to present. Accept simply that my purpose was and is to express the truth of God . . . that He is only Love, and so are you.

At what precise moment did you know that you had achieved the fullness of the Christ?

You are seeking an answer to a question in terms of time, and I will give you an answer reflective of the same. It was at the moment that I allowed myself to be consciously released from the cross. The answer that will be more meaningful for you, however, will be this: the moment when I knew there was no need to either be attached to or released from the cross, that was the moment that I could let all illusion go.

Did you experience pain when you were on the cross?

I was not totally in possession of my identity as the Christ at each and every moment I was in the physical embodiment. There were times when I did experience pain as I identified myself with the body that was hanging on the cross.

If you were to ask for a simple definition or explanation as to when did I recognize that I am the Christ, and when I was out of that recognition, one very simple way to describe it would be if I felt pain, if I felt anything that did not reflect the joy that is the Presence of God, I was not in recognition of my Self. Suffering of any nature, be it physical or mental, is not the domain of God. It is not the wish of God to test anyone as to the depths of his capability to withstand suffering. It is only the wish of God for you and I to experience the Essence of that which He Is. And I will tell you that there is no pain, there is no suffering in the Mind of God. There you will find joy, and there you will find peace, and there you will find only Love.

Choices made to experience suffering and pain are simply experiences that will ultimately prove to you that they have been choices made apart from the Will of God. You will recognize your will and the Creator's Will as being in absolute synchrony when you do not even consider choices that bring you anything other than peace and joy.

Tom:

During a conversation I had with a friend about Jesus life, he asked if I was aware, or had been told, if or when he had reached the moment of awakening to the truth about himself. As he was asking the question I began to see the setting of the crucifixion. There were four crosses; one was empty. Many people were gathered at the site. Some were close, most were at a distance as if unsure about being seen there. It was an overcast but very still day.

As I mentally "watched," I was aware that he was floating in and out of physical consciousness, but his mind was fully at peace. It felt as if he wasn't really "there." I also was aware that I was anticipating that what I was going to "see" was a kind of flash of light and he would disappear. I did then see the flash of light, but it remained and filled my vision. I realized then it was the world that had disappeared from his mind.

The symbolism was perfectly clear. What was real was unchanged. When he had awakened to the truth, the thought of sin and a world of separateness that was not real had left his mind and the experience of it simply ceased to be. What a perfect illustration of what he teaches.

Why could you not have chosen an easier way to demonstrate infinite life? Could not your purpose have been fulfilled in a less drastic, a less violent way? Why did you not continue teaching, loving, expressing, living out a so-called "normal life span" and make the transition in a less painful way?

The moment to experience the fulfillment of my purpose was then at hand. Why the cross? People will understand language that is spoken in terms of the time they perceive themselves being enmeshed in. While my purpose may have been fulfilled in another fashion, it would not have served the dual purpose I had intended. Thus, I allowed it to proceed in terms that had been set in motion by the mood of the time.

I have said before that many questions are answered but not heard, because the focus of the listener was not in atunement with the way that the answer was presented. The emotion and perception of that time was served most appropriately by the event as it occurred. This does not mean, or should not be reflective of, anyone else's needing to make a decision to find and experience their Christhood in terms that would be anything other than peaceful and loving.

My understanding is that you then appeared after the resurrection in the order of love that you had shared with those individuals. Is this correct?

This is a misperception based upon a need to place characters close to my person in order of importance. My attempts to convey my understanding about myself and my Father were always directed toward establishing each person as an integral and equal aspect of the Love of God and always in equal receipt of the Love of God. Would you not then find it to be totally contradictory for me to appear to one whom I said I loved most, thereby in some way relegating my love for another to a lesser stature? This was not so.

There were many misunderstandings at the time. I will tell you this: many more saw me than what has been recorded, and saw me at a time and at a place that seemingly occurred after the moment of my death. I would like you to understand that because of the nature of the purpose that was to be fulfilled—that being the illustration of an infinite life—those who asked and who believed and for whom purpose was fulfilled to see a facsimile of the physical embodiment being recreated, were answered. The sequence in which these requests were made and answered bore no relevance to my feelings for any of those involved.

Was this facsimile a higher energy state than the dense level of our normal physical form?

It might surprise you to note that it was different in different cases. In each case, however, the purpose for which the vision or sighting was necessary was fulfilled, and whatever method was necessary for its fulfillment took place quite naturally.

How did you manifest yourself for Thomas?

His request was made from a feeling of needing confirmation, not so much based upon a need to understand a continuation of his Life Force or my Life Force, but was based upon a feeling of accepting the love that I spoke to him about. He felt this had been removed as my physical presence was removed. It was in response to this need that I appeared to him. And just to satisfy your curiosity in terms that you describe as being dense, it was quite a dense manifestation. It was one that was designed to leave as little room for doubt as possible, and in that regard, there was additional physical contact made.

I always wondered why you never had any women within your circle?

There were many women within my circle. There were far more women within my circle than has been reported or recorded. At the time recordation was being made, it was not acceptable. I will assure you that I had many brothers and many sisters of whom the records make no account. Nor is it necessary that they do so.

May I ask why there were no women disciples? Was it because they would not have been listened to, given the cultural standards of the time?

It was purely a social implication, and yes, you are correct. They would indeed not have been listened to at that time. The other implications revolved around the caring for the family. Women were at the very center and core of family care.

Allow me to speak to another issue. You give far too much importance in your mind to the role of the disciples as being the carriers or bearers of our mutual teachings. The sharings that you have in your own life are quite meaningful and fulfilling to both you and those around you. It is the nature and intimacy of these sharings that was even more at the core of what was happening in my relationships at that particular time. And in that regard, I will tell you there were many relationships with women; much time shared, much love shared, and much mutual benefit derived, not only from my direct relationships with women at that time, but with those that these women subsequently encountered. Much of this encountering took place within the core of family units and it was within this context that their purpose had great meaning.

Many have wondered about the eighteen years between your appearance in Nazareth and your baptism in the River Jordan. What were you doing during that time?

There were many travels. There were multitudes of experiences, but to more succinctly answer your question, I was fulfilling my role as being the man, Jesus. I was calling to me the experiences that would, in fact, bring me to a point of allowing myself to have the full recognition of the Christ, which I previously described to you as having been experienced at the moment upon leaving the cross.

Please do not try to differentiate, or hold in any form, a special meaning to the journey that I was on as opposed to the journey that you are on. To say that my attempts for understanding and learning were on a higher level than yours, or were on a plane which exceeded your understanding, would be extremely unhelpful.

You see, there is no depth to understanding. There is no distance between you and the acceptance of your Being. That too, is a vast misperception. To allow your thinking to dwell in this area would say to you it is possible to lengthen the distance between yourself and God. And I will tell you that is in no way possible. There is only your perception of how far away from your Self you are in any given moment, and at any given moment should you so choose to completely abandon your sense of isolation, and totally embrace your sense of being the extension of your Father, then it will be so and it will be so instantaneously.

Do not dwell upon me as having been an example for you in light of my seemingly achieving what I did in a relatively short number of years. Your process and my process were different processes, but the results are inevitably the same. At the moment I chose to let go, I recognized that I had never left my Father's Home, and the moment you choose to let go—completely, totally—you will recognize the same. How each of us arrives at that point of allowing the decision to come is totally and utterly irrelevant. I did what needed best to be done for me to illustrate that fact, and you simply need to know that you are doing the same.

I am no greater Son of God than you are. I occupy no special space in His Heart which is above and beyond that which you occupy.

His Purpose

I shared with someone that your primary purpose for being on earth at that time was to take on or achieve the fullness of the Christ. He asked then if you didn't also have a teaching purpose or ministry. Is that true?

If you recognize yourself as being in a state of Love and when you hear the request of a brother asking you to express your Love, is it so difficult to recognize that this is what was happening to me? To fulfill my purpose, the process was one of sharing my insights and guidance with those who were around me. That has become known as a ministry.

There is often the attempt made to draw conclusions based upon information which has previously been presented as to the form and the function that the sharing took. When you do not make comparisons and draw conclusions based upon past judgments, your understanding will then be much clearer. Simply direct a question with an open mind towards seeking information which you believe will be helpful to you now. If your question was, "Were you a teacher during that period of time," my answer would be," Yes." I would also tell you that I was a student. I would tell you that I shared the insights and the knowing that I had at the moment with those around me because they were important to me, and they were important to the process of my knowing who I was.

But the path that I had chosen should not be judged by any other to necessarily be appropriate for them. Nor should my path in any way become a basis for judgment about the path that they are currently on. This consistently results in the continuation of the misperception that I am different from you. Not only different, but that I am better than you. The more concrete this belief becomes, the more difficult it obviously is for you to recognize our equality, but more importantly to recognize that no one exists within the Christ who is in any way elevated above the whole or any aspect of the whole.

If you were to believe that any single expression of the Christ held a special place within the Christ, then you must ultimately draw the conclusion that there would be many special beings. And if there are many others who are higher, then there must of necessity be many others who are lower, and I will guarantee you that you will put yourself on the lowest rung of the ladder and that is not our purpose. Our purpose is to recognize the Love of God and recognize ourselves as being the expression of the Love of God and not to see one as being more capable of expressing it than any other.

I experienced something that I don't understand completely. While sitting at the dinner table, I was thinking about the crucifixion and asking myself, why did Jesus have to suffer on the cross, why did this have to happen? Jesus, nailed to the cross, then appeared on the table across from me. I asked him, "Why did you let this happen?" He did not answer, but he sat up, reached over and hugged me, the cross bending around me with his hands still nailed to it. I told this experience to others only two times and each time I cried uncontrollably. I could not stop or prevent the crying.

Could you explain this experience so that it would be helpful to me?

My dear brother, I would suggest you allow this experience to come to you one more time with this subtle change: as you feel the embrace, see the cross drop away. It is indeed your symbolism of the cross that brings you the feeling of pain and anguish, and it is that anguish that hides the joyous feeling that was meant by the embrace.

You asked the question, "Why did you need to do this?" and I would like to say to you, do not confuse your path with mine. Do not imagine that because of your perception of me and what I achieved on the path I followed to remembering the truth that we are that the same path is appropriate for you. Those experiences that I needed to bring me to the full realization of truth were chosen by me in a way that best illustrated my purpose given the circumstances that existed then. They would be absolutely irrelevant to your situation and circumstances as they exist now.

I call you "Brother" to help you understand that I am not above you. I hope that you will realize there was nothing special or significant in the choices that I made as they would pertain to the choices that you make. I urge you not to focus on my process. Do not allow yourself to become buried in the thoughts that are brought to your mind by seeing me nailed to a cross. For I will tell you that you have nailed yourself to many crosses, and while they appear to be different, they are not.

While the anguish that you suffer appears to be less intense than the anguish you perceive that I suffered, it is not so. It is time now for you to give up the cross, both yours and mine.

Allow the feelings of the embrace, the Love that we share, to be that which you identify with. Please no longer misunderstand the message that was given you by the feeling, by the picture, by the interpretations of others as I seemingly was sent to death to endure pain for the purpose of "relieving you of sins." These are misperceptions. Understand the Love that I hold for you. Understand also, that I could not hold this Love for you if I did not feel it coming from you, if I could not know that Love was the identification of your Being.

You have a question about what happened to my body. I will tell you that there is a thought in your mind that you would hold out this mysterious disappearance of the physical remains of my body as being some type of clue to your achieving your Divinity in a like fashion. And this is not necessary. I will give you an explanation physiologically that will satisfy your curiosity. It is simply this: your body and my body are nothing more than the manifestations that our mind encompasses for them. There will be a time when this mystery no longer exists for you. As you wish to manifest a body or to allow it to return to a non-physical element, it will simply be so, because you understand that this is the nature of it. But I will tell you that at this moment, it would be a power that would be identifiable to you as a magical trick that your ego could perform to illustrate a type of superiority. Within that purpose, it would not then be helpful for you to hold this illustration. What is important for you to understand is that the body itself was irrelevant. I do not say unimportant; I say irrelevant.

Whatever experiences you have chosen to have at any given moment, all that is necessary to implement those experiences you will automatically have. As you are now within a range of experiences illustrated by physical expression, you now have a body that will aid in those experiences. As you choose a range of experiences where a physical body or any other physical materialization would be unnecessary, then you will not have the experience of those things being physical. That is why it is simply irrelevant. I ask you to honor the choices that you are making and, therefore, to honor the tools which aid in those choices. But do not identify yourself, your Self of Being, as in any way being identified by that physical expression.

Your focus, your attention at this time, is most helpfully centered upon experiencing the love and the joy that you have been denying yourself. Just that.

It will be in your choices for this change of attitude that you will less harshly judge yourself and return to a state of Knowing. I simply say to you, be at peace. And I encourage you to know, as you allow your experience of our being together to enter your mind again, that we are together and that we can be in a state of communion at that moment, as we are now. Should you decide to make this choice, then just allow it to be so with the full understanding that it will be.

I would like to know about your relationship with your earthly father, Joseph, and the Being that he is now.

My relationship with my father as I was in a physical body was an exceptional one. It was one of total acceptance. I'm sure you can recognize how difficult it would be if you had a child who did the things that historically you have read that I did. It was not difficult in our case. My father was, indeed, an open mind. And that open mind readily absorbed what was happening and it was not at all a shock to him. There were many things he did not understand; there were only very, very few which he found difficult to accept. It was to my vast benefit to have been in this environment of unconditional allowing. My preparation, my becoming aware of who I am, was enhanced by his loving presence. I presented many conflicts to the existing ideologies, and my father was a deeply religious person. It was to his great credit that he did not perceive the conflicts that I presented to the ideologies as being conflicts reflective of himself, of his role as a parent. He uniquely flowed. And he uniquely flows this day.

Our relationship was not what you would consider to be closely personal as I approached the age of puberty. This was a result of my own struggles, my own efforts to find myself. And it left me less room, so to speak, for personal relationships. He was also quite aware of this. And while he did not know at that time—as I did not know—what was to come, his faith was of such a nature that he trusted in an outcome which he knew would be absolutely perfect for the two of us.

The Second Coming

Would you please explain the process of the "Second Coming?" I feel that is the returning to our consciousness of the Christ awareness, but there has been another understanding which says that you, Jesus, physically will be returning.

I have no plans at the moment.

Do you have any plans in the future?

I ask you to live in the moment. Will you not allow me the same prerogative?

Your perception is quite correct. The misperception is the one that says there was a first or a second coming. The Christ has never changed. Should you say, "Will the Jesus-person be coming again," it would be totally different in its meaning. Whether or not the Jesus-person returns should be looked upon by you as being totally irrelevant. There are many reasons for this. Why would I encourage you to understand that, on the one hand, simply because we appear to be in different states of embodiment, we are not really separate, and then encourage you to look forward to my coming again which would indicate to you that this would somehow bring us closer?

You are attempting to allow your mind slowly and gently to transcend the thoughts of limitation. It would not be appropriate for me to act in any way that would be contradictory to what you are doing. I will say to you as well that speaking in terms of the Christ, it is also irrelevant if there is a "Second Coming." There is only one point of value and that is for you to recognize at this moment, what Is. At this moment, you Are. You are in a state of being the Christ, of being the expression of God who expresses Himself as being You. I ask you only to recognize this. How could it be important to allow your attention to dwell upon any second coming? There is no value to you there.

The Present

Why have you chosen to be with us at this particular time and space?

There is no time and there is no space, and I have no choice except to be with you because we are inseparable. There is no other special dimension that you, at this moment, are capable of conceiving. It is not vast, it is not small; it is. It cannot be known as a dimension because that would place a limitation upon it. Nor can it be known as being so vast that you cannot conceive of yourself filling it up. These are games that will only entertain your ego-mind. I suggest that you simply accept what I have said: there is no time, there is no space, there is no way for us to be apart because the Mind of God is whole. Within that wholeness lies the Mind of His Son, and neither is separate from the other or from any infinite aspect of Itself as it is expressed. Do not attempt to conceptualize this in terms that you would relate to physical boundaries— it cannot be done. For the moment, allow yourself just the awareness of what I have said because it is.

Is there anything else you would like to share at this time?

The Love that is present within you is a wondrous thing to share. It is your sharing of this Love that is the most significant thing you do. Again, it becomes a matter of allowing the *feeling* to become the focus. Words can be perceived and misperceived, but they are at all times within the realm of perception. It is when you allow yourself to become fully immersed in the feeling of your Being, in the feeling of Love, that you will communicate to others who God Is. When you try to rationally explain what it is you feel a need to do, it is precisely this: to communicate the Love of God. This will not happen with words.

Chapter Six

Illusion versus Reality

"Because you experience only those things that are in your mind, when you have accepted Reality, it is all you will experience."

Freedom From Illusion

As you begin your pursuit of this journey called Awakening, there is a tendency to become confused over issues of responsibility. You must keep a clear picture in your mind of what you have made versus the Real world, the world that is the extension of the Mind of God. As I have spoken to you before about changing your mind and your perception about what is going on, you may find it extremely difficult to do this if you are under the impression that any of the things that I ask you to change your perception of are felt by you to be the domain of God. And, therefore, you put yourself in a position of feeling that there is nothing you can really do about it.

Let me begin with this illustration: Look about you and allow your attention to encompass all of the things you can see. These are things with form. And this form that you are experiencing through your physical senses is of *your* creation. The thoughts and feelings you have about these forms totally determine what they mean to you and this is what I refer to as perception. Behind these forms, the *essence* of these forms is the extension of, the reality of, the Mind of God. And that is why I can say to you all that needs to be done is to change this perception, allowing yourself to come into a more accurate awareness of the reality of that which you perceive. I do not ask you to discard your creation or to regard it in any manner as being an illusion, as lacking reality. What I am attempting to direct your attention to is a clearer, more truthful recognition of that which you are perceiving. And it is in this light that I ask you to step beyond the illusion, beyond the perception that is bounded with fear and guilt and judgment and to see through your natural eyes.

The most common illustration of which I am speaking is the matter of your own body and the sickness and death that occurs to and within that body. As I have said, all of the meaning of the physical form is generated within your mind. And when that mind encompasses a belief system which allows the presence of pain and accepts the deterioration to death, then that will be your experience of your body. Lest there be a misunderstanding, I will state quite clearly: the physical body that you possess is of *your own* creation and it is created by your thought system to conform to the meaning you have given it. It will function according to the laws, if you will, that are the reflections of your own beliefs. I would also have you know there is no other object or form that is present in your perception to which this same concept does not apply. *It is totally impossible for you to experience any form in a way other than that which conforms to your belief system.* It is always within the scope of this truth that I encourage you to change your perception, to change the way you look at the form which you think you see surrounding you.

That is why I continuously say there is truly nothing happening around you that is not first happening in your mind. And to effect a change of any nature in those things, it is only necessary to change your mind. The difficulty of this process is determined largely upon how completely and thoroughly you accept what I have just stated.

Whenever you are faced with a question about whether or not you can, in fact, change anything around you because it is of your making or if that thing has been created by God and is, therefore, changeless, ask yourself this:

1. Is that thing which I am questioning eternal?

2. Is it limitless?

3. Is it possible for me to experience all aspects of this in a way that is loving?

4. In each and every circumstance, is my being resonant with this thing bringing me a sense of absolute peace?

If the answer to any of these questions is no, then be certain that your perception of it is quite out of alignment with its reality, and all that needs to be changed is the way that you view it. Were it not so, then you must believe that God would have created you a prisoner. He would have created you locked in a cage of death and pain, and you know this is not so. The cage of pain and death are your miscreations merely by the perception within which you view them. And your freedom lies in your decision to truly recognize your Self.

I suggest to you that within this information lies all the freedom you would seek.

I am not suggesting, however, that you specifically use only the four criteria stated as a hard and fast test. These are suggestions. They are valid and they will work, but programming your mind to allow these four things to be the sieve through which you run all things before you understand whether they are truth or illusion is setting up something that is not helpful to you in the long run. The idea is to take these principles and get the *feel* of them, so that your mind then has this general comprehension of how you go about testing for truth versus illusion.

Are you saying that when faced with the choice of active involvement protesting situations such as the endangered environment or nuclear weapons, that we have made these situations by our perceptions and we can just as easily unmake them by changing our mind and recognizing them as illusions?

Again, bear in mind the illusion is the distorted way you perceive that which is of Creation. The illusion is your miscreation which overlays the reality and the clarity as expressed and extended through the Mind of God. There is nothing but perfection and truth that is resonant in the Mind of God. That which is not seen or recognized as being perfection and truth has been misperceived as an illusion of truth. And it is the correction of this perception that I encourage you to make.

For me to tell you that it is not helpful for many people to protest an illusion they have made would be equally false. The way in which each individual protests, if you will, the illusion of his creation depends upon that path which will bring the reality of what is happening most easily and clearly to his attention. That which is not helpful is to believe that what you are protesting has influence over you . . . that you are the victim of it. The meaning you have given that which you are protesting is all the meaning it has. It exists as the effect of your perception of it. What it amounts to is that you are protesting you own beliefs.

Changing illusions is something that anyone will attempt to do who has chosen to be on the path of Awakening. Some will pursue it by openly and actively challenging the physical manifestation of the illusion, because that appears most likely to them as the way to get their attention. Ultimately, as we have just discussed, there is but one way to change illusion, and that is to change your perception of it. That change comes only from changing your mind. My suggestion to you would be to not concern yourself with any procedural attempts that are made by others in the manner or fashion which they have decided to protest their illusion. To do so keeps your mind in a state of judgment and your attention away from your own path of changing the way you think about your illusion.

Would you say then in accordance with the procedure of Awakening, the highest and best thing we can do is to simply see these issues as illusion and to not be involved with them?

The highest and best way for you might be quite different from the highest and best way for another. I would advise you not to establish what I would call a dogma about the process of Awakening. Please remember, there are as many paths to God as those who seek Him. To know what is right for you, learn to ask.

Seeing Reality

If we have made forms by the process of our thoughts, have we also made the natural forces such as the wind and the mountains, the trees and the oceans?

The issue that concerns you which you are addressing with this question, is whether or not many of the natural forces that you see about you are of God, or is it your perception of them which you are viewing. All of the natural forces that you see about you are of God, because they contain the energy that is the extension of His Thought. But the way you perceive these forces, the form you perceive them to be in, the purpose and function you give them, imposes limitation and distorts your experience of them.

Looking at the natural world, I see everything going through decay and death. Creatures die, that's not a bad thing, just a pattern of life. Is this merely perception or is it a larger plan of the Creation process?

You have explained why you experience death and decay happening as you describe the process as "just a pattern of life." You have accepted it as being real and therefore, it appears to you in that fashion. Do not confuse cause with effect. I was not advocating eternal physical expression when I described to you the truth that nothing manifests for you physically that is not a product of your belief system. In fact, once you totally accept this truth, you will find that you no longer have a fear of releasing your hold on the body because you will know that it is not the identification of you. What I have described is your passage to this freedom.

I know that it is quite difficult to understand that as you see birds and plants dying, they are dying because of your belief system, they are dying because you are seeing them die. Once you have lifted the veil of identifying them and yourself as being perishable, you will no longer experience that which you have identified as the process of death.

Is the reality of that which we perceive as death something has not ended, but has simply changed form?

You determine the meaning of the form you "see" by your perception of what is real for you. Seeing through and beyond the limitation of these beliefs allows you to see the form in its reality which is infinite. You will not then even perceive a change in form, because the form will no longer be the object of your focus. You will experience the changeless, the absolutely infinite expression of the Mind of God. There is nothing created by God, which is the expression and the extension of the Mind of God, that is changeable. There is no need to alter perfection.

As your fundamental belief in guilt and fear changes, it won't be a matter of seeing energy change form; you won't experience the illusion of forms. You will not experience war nor will you see war; you will not experience death or confusion or chaos in any form. As it leaves your mind, it *must* also leave your experience.

Will it be in other people's field of experience, but my perception will have just changed so much that I will see it differently?

This is part of the general concept of thinking that there is yourself and somebody else and that there are two different things going on. As long as you seek to verify your own experiences by looking to see what's going on with somebody else, you miss the point. All that is happening is that you are accepting their experience as opposed to having the benefit of your own.

I know that this is one of the most difficult things for you to accept. Once you have changed your mind about what you wish to experience, anything in opposition to your new belief will no longer be present in your experience. It will not be a matter of rising above it or understanding how somebody else is perceiving it. *You will not see it.* It will not be happening. You will not be aware that there is a war going on and some people are buying into it and you are not; you will not experience war.

Then how do you communicate with those people who are?

You already are. You are constantly communicating with people who are experiencing totally different perceptions than you are. Because you only experience those things that are in your mind, when you have accepted Reality, it is all you will experience.

And you will communicate beautifully with all of your Awakened friends. But it is a matter of accepting a truth in its totality and not just that part of it which comfortably fits into an intellectual niche at the moment. When you accept the precept that you will experience nothing except that which is a reflection of your thought system, you must understand that this statement is totally true. There is no exception for how you would be communicating with people who were not in that same thought system. You will not experience other people feeling or thinking differently than that which conforms to this new thought pattern.

So we will experience other people conforming to our thought patterns. Everything will make the shift. Everything in our thought system, every reflection of it, will undergo a complete shift.

That's a very good way to describe it.

It seems to me that at some point I made the choice to move into the level of Reality, but that I won't meet my own criteria for making the move until I have come back all the way to this level of illusion.

Your real fear is that if you stay in Reality you'll be all alone.

That's it exactly.

There is no way for you to be alone in the experience of Reality. You take everything in your consciousness with you. You only see it differently. You see it more accurately as being a reflection of your whole Self. The only thing you leave behind is the limited perception of it, the illusory thinking that gave it an unreal characteristic.

There was a fear that if I totally committed to leaving this dimension, I would feel myself separate from everything else.

If you think that coming back to this frame of reference brought you a feeling of being connected to those around you, you have forgotten the experience of the feeling of connection that takes place when you transcend that fear of being alone. When you have accepted your unification with the Mind of God, you will discover it was a place you never really left, which obviously means no one else did either.

An Image Given Tom:

> *I'm getting a picture of you holding hands in a circle of people dancing around and being very gleeful and laughing and happy. You have flowers in your hair and are in a meadow. And then I have this other image of the same thing taking place on what we are perceiving as a second, higher level. Here on the higher level there is just this wonderful flowing of light that just swirls and intermingles. You don't see where one light stops and the other one starts, it just flows. And now I'm seeing this lower circle of dancers stop and some pair off and go in one direction and others in other directions. They form new circles and start to do other dances, but on the higher level, none of the flowing of light changes, it remains constant. The feeling is that as happy and as connected as we can be on the lower level you are aware of your differences, but on the level of experiencing your Self there is never a feeling of polarity, or difference, or opposite. It is a constant state of the same flow.*

The reason for seeing the two levels of dancing was to illustrate that we only pretend that we are dancing " here." That's the illusion, that we're here doing the dance instead of the reality that we're "there" doing the dance. That is why you cannot be alone. This is the only place you can seem to be alone.

Time

There must be something that I am hanging onto which may be the reason that I came back into the body and is the reason why I don't now feel Awake. Can you help me with what that is?

At this particular moment, you are looking for a reason so that you would have something else to work on, another problem to solve, and that would not be the most helpful thing to do. Working on your problems only focuses more of your attention and emotion on the issues you want to get rid of. This will have the opposite effect you hope to achieve. The more you energize the issue with attention and emotion, the more intense it will become.

I do not suggest that you ignore or resist any problem you perceive you have. Rather it is a process of looking at it, allowing it to speak to you and then pass away. You become able to allow it to go by reminding yourself who you are and letting go of the value you have previously placed on the underlying fear. Both resisting and working on the problem emphasize the control you acknowledge it has over you. Being able to look at it and dismiss it is a disavowal of the illusion of being self victimized and an acknowledgment of your Divinity. Additionally, there exists a small fear that develops on the edge of one of your barriers that says, "I think I understand, but I don't really want to have to come back around time and time again." Let go of the concept of time.

I don't understand how to do that.

There is no framework, no parameter of time within which you must achieve your Awakening.

But I don't want to keep coming back.

You see, that's the dichotomy I was describing. To work on becoming Awakened now to avoid having to continue to return gives validity to the concept of time and acknowledges its control over you, and this only keeps it in your awareness and consequently in your experience. As you remain as consistently as possible in the current instant, the concept of time takes on a different meaning until, at last, it goes away. You are infinite. Time is but a figment of your imagination. It is at *your* disposal. Literally.

Is part of the process of waking up then understanding that there is no time and just trying to always be in the present moment?

Letting go of all concepts which contain limitation will allow your mind to be more receptive to the flooding in of the information, the memory, of who you truly Are. It is most difficult for that memory to return to a space in which it appears to be in conflict. It is most difficult for your memory of you as an infinite Being to return to a mind that believes in time, which believes that there are barriers of any nature, limitations of any kind which separate you from the Mind of God and from every brother and sister around you.

Do not dwell on how to let go of a concept such as time, or anything else which appears to you as a boundary. Just understand that there are none. Don't give your ego additional opportunities to take up a banner of defending time. Just let them go. Don't try to understand at this moment why you cannot let go, or why they do not apply to you; just know that they do not, and let them go. The unlimited reality of your Self will then fill the space that is revealed to you which then becomes acceptable to your thinking as you remove the concepts of limitation.

It is impossible for you to grasp my meaning when I tell you there is no separation between your mind and the limitless Mind of God as long as you see yourself as being identified by your body, having fears and anxieties and experiencing the things that limited thinking brings to you. I encourage you to simply let go of the concept that there are any boundaries around you.

So for now, just allow the notion to be present that we have no boundaries, no limitations at all. And with that understanding, watch and see how many new definitions and recognitions of your Self will become apparent to you . . . how much more of the information that I give you will now be understood and acceptable to you.

Divine Indifference?

I get lost in trying to understand the "Divine indifference" of God, or being in a state of "beyond it all." Could you talk about that?

I cannot render any meaningful description of indifference as in any way being Divine. A state of Divinity as it exists within you and within the Mind of God is in no way indifferent. The peaceful state of seeing only that which truly exists is not one which could be described as indifferent. What you are referring to is a state of not caring which exists only in a mind as it is occupied within the illusion.

There is a statement which you are familiar with from *A Course in Miracles* that expresses the fact that the Father does not recognize the illusion within which you recognize yourself as currently being. This is not indicative of any indifference on His part. It is merely an indication that He does not wish to dream.

There is an act of honoring choices made within the illusion for the value which they will have to help extricate you from the illusion. This is not an act of indifference nor of being uncaring. It is more aptly described as being in recognition of that which is illusion as opposed to that which sees Reality. I see Reality as being only the extension of the Mind and Love of God. And in that extension, I see only peace and perfection and harmony. If my brother is not experiencing that vision, and I refuse to share his not seeing it, I am not indifferent. I am more truthfully putting myself in a state of supporting Reality as opposed to supporting illusion. I can feel in no way indifferent as I express the unconditional Love that is the extension of the Mind of God.

Should I show concern for the fact that anyone else is not currently experiencing that sense of peace, then I am, on the one hand, not honoring his right of free choice, and on the other, not honoring my choice to experience only that which is real. And this in no way constitutes being indifferent.

So what does it mean to "save the world?"

You save the world by changing your vision to see it as it really is. You restore the world's sanity by reclaiming your right Mind, altering your vision to see that which is reflective of the Mind of God. The only way to save the world is to change the meaning you have imposed upon it. Because you see yourself in a state of limitation, it is difficult to understand that the view you hold of your brother is also an illusion of his real Self. As your perception changes, the world and everything in it correspondingly must shift to reflect your new beliefs.

I don't understand what you mean when you say, "as I see myself in a state of limitation."

As you see yourself occupying a space which has boundaries and draws a distinction between your space and the space occupied by another, you are seeing a world which is compartmentalized, divided up into little pieces and segments. What I am presenting to you is a world quite different from this. It is a world of energetic wholeness. It is one in which there are no divisions between expressions of God, one in which there is a total blending because that blending, in fact, expresses the harmony that is the whole of Creation.

So can the nature of my feeling loving be anything but illusory?

The illusory aspect of love that you are currently experiencing is one of feeling a need to project it, so that you will recognize that love has indeed come from you. That is an illusion. To recognize that you are in a state of being Love, that it is the only state in which you truly exist and, therefore, is the only thing that is possible for you to extend, is to be in a state of recognizing the Love which is of Reality, of your Self. When you feel a *need* to project love, you are in a state of mind that believes that you can create love, and it is this state of mind that would also convince you that you can create something that is not love—that Love would have an opposite. It is this type of love that is reflective of your being in a dream.

When you recognize yourself as being an expression of the act of Love, which is the creative force of All That Is and is the expression of its Creator, then you will recognize yourself as being Love and being an extension of the Mind of God. And you will know that it is quite impossible for you to be anything else. It is when you do not see this that you are seeing an illusion of Reality and of your Self.

Special Relationships

What is the value and significance of an intimate, committed relationship between a man and a woman?

I would say to you that there is relatively little difference between the value of the relationship you describe and the value of any other relationship you would have on a more casual basis. What does happen, however, is that an intimate relationship forces you to acknowledge your reaction to a given individual on a continuous basis without the opportunity to back away.

By way of explanation, the value of any relationship is that which is achieved as you allow yourself to express only love. If you take this answer and apply it to what I have said about an intimate relationship, you can see how that learning takes on what appears to be impossible proportions at times, given the nature of not being able to back away. The other thing that happens is that within an intimate relationship dependencies are built. And with dependency comes the accompanying fear as to what will happen if the dependency is no longer available to you. This would appear to complicate even further your ability to always extend the act of an uncompromising and unconditionally loving response to each and every situation that occurs.

The nature of your question, however, is not directed toward the dissection of how a happy relationship is generated between two who are intimate with each other, but more toward an attempt to understand whether or not there is a broader purpose to be achieved within that relationship than in a relationship that is not intimate. My answer to that is no. There is no broader purpose. There is no greater value. It is simply a matter that within the intimacy, because of the accompanying complexities which personalities and emotions generate, an intimate relationship appears to be more significant. And as you view it as being more significant, then the attention you pay to it and the value you give to it will appear to take on greater proportions.

Please speak of the significance, if any, of sexual love.

It would be most difficult to generalize and have your information be reflective of the truth. Sexual love may be experienced and may have its value in allowing yourself to remove barriers against being intimate on a more knowing level. Or, it may take on the significance that is reflective of a fear that you hold about yourself.

Any act or emotion that is expressed by you, be it sexual or not, is reflective of the state of mind that you are in at the moment. And if the state of mind is one that is free and does not contain a fearful base, then that act or emotion will be expressed in a fashion which is more reflective of your being in a state of truth. So I would suggest that you do not distinguish or differentiate between a sexual act or any other emotional act that you may feel yourself involved in at any given moment. If it expresses love, it will bring you peace.

Much has been said about the sexual drive as being an excuse to continue the human species. As long as you see yourself as a Being that needs to be reproduced through this process and this becomes your understanding, then that will be the urge to which you will respond. And you will recognize your sex drive as simply being that. I would call to your attention that this same logic could be applied to war. As your thinking process encompasses the belief that you have a basis for being fearful and must, therefore, protect yourself, you will engage in conflict. You will feel an urge or a driving need to be defensive.

What I am simply presenting to you here is the understanding that you will respond to whatever your belief system dictates. If that system should tell you that the expression of sex is an expression of love, then that is the way you will experience it. If it should tell you that it is in response to a need to fulfill a physical function, then that is what you will respond to. It is no different than the other emotions you have and find a need to express.

The Depths of Illusion

I have had the experience of recognizing truth that I have heard come through you and it feels so wonderful. But how is it that others are equally convinced that they know the truth and my truth is wrong?

Let us first return to the very fundamental question of right and wrong, good and bad, up and down, in and out, illusion and truth. You know that these are concepts you play with while you are asleep. So who is dreaming a better dream? Are there degrees of being Awake?

There is a perception that you have varying depths of illusions, but I would bring your memory back to a statement I have made that said, in actuality, there is illusion and no illusion. Please don't misunderstand that. I don't mean that in Reality there is an illusion, but where you are, you are either experiencing illusion or you are not. That being an extremely difficult pill to swallow, your ego allows you to continue accomplishing things by giving you permission to slowly come out of the illusion. And that is what I referred to when I said that in your perception, there is a depth to the illusion. Now, let's go back to the original question and I would ask you, what is your motive for wanting to know?

My ego's frustration, I suppose. Why don't we all recognize the same truth?

I have said many times that there is no difference in any brother's ability to recognize truth. Whether or not you choose to exercise that ability is another in a long list of choices that you may or may not make. You find the search for truth to be very satisfying. I will tell you that there are many to whom the search for truth is quite terrifying and it is not because they are afraid of finding truth. It is because there are too many layers of other fears which they translate into a fear of death, and I am not simply referring to death on a physical level. There are many who do not yet understand, truly understand, that it is impossible to die, that there is not a vengeful God who can and would take away their infinite life. Their struggle appears to be different from yours, but I would remind you that struggle is struggle and it is all maintained within the illusion.

I suggest that it would be quite helpful to shift from looking upon the perceived state of mind of these brothers as being one of unwillingness to find and hear truth, as you perceive it, to one of recognizing who they really are. You can spend a great deal of time feeling pain for them, or judging them, which does nothing more than keep your eyes in darkness. I tell you again, *you* are Awake. I tell you now, *they* are also Awake, and I would ask you to see them as so. This not only facilitates their own awakening but you would be amazed at what it does for yours.

I'm not sure how to do that.

In each case that we discuss, what we are concerning ourselves with is seeing beyond the illusion, building a mind pattern which allows us to see beyond the illusion in every event. It is a process that becomes acceptable to you, that slowly allows you to feel more Awake. Let's take a very simple analogy: You have many wondrous bananas growing on your trees. If one day you should decide to call them apples and continue to call them apples for a long period of time, they would become apples to you. And then it would take a whole new mind pattern of getting you back into the groove of calling them bananas.

There is no one in your dimension who is not trying to wake up. You find this very difficult to accept because your mind immediately brings forth all of those "terribly bad people"; the murderers, the rapists, the terrorists, and so forth. But I will remind you that at the deepest level, there is no one who does not wish to return to his natural state. There is no one within whom the memory does not exist in which the certainty of the peace and the harmony that reflects their Being does not reside as a call to come Home.

You have established a belief pattern as to the depth of the illusion and it is within that pattern, your giving credence to that pattern, that you see others and yourself as being relatively asleep. And yet I would ask you as you go to sleep within the dream and have sleeping dreams within the greater dream and believe these to be real, do you not think that same condition exists with every other brother? And do you think that you wake up from your dreams any differently than they? It's simply a matter that the dreams are different, but they are dreams. And when the fear becomes overwhelming in the dream, the desire to wake up is recognized more clearly.

Each brother appears to hear his wake up call quite differently. Indeed, you would think it apparent that some have not even asked!

When I encounter those who insist that the banana is an apple, do I just say nothing, or do I . . .

You continue to be the banana, for this is the only true form they will recognize.

It's not the words . . . .

Truly.

Chapter Seven

Being in the Present

"If being in the moment is an expression of your natural state of Being, then it must, in its truest essence, be an easy act."

Staying in the Present

I am attempting to discover what it means to live in the now. It feels like part of me is holding onto the past and part of me is hanging onto the future, so I've never really experienced being fully present. How can I do that?

Remaining in the "now" is a struggle because you feel there is much in the past that you still value. And since you cannot yet conceive of yourself as an infinite Being, without a past you would not seem to exist. In order to take the struggle out of remaining in the present, you must come to see that what you value from the past arose from your thoughts of guilt and fear. Saying this, I do not exclude those memories of love and joy that you do not now understand were but a fraction of what they would have been, unencumbered by your fearful beliefs.

In this experience of a world that comes from your current confused and conflicted awareness, it is impossible for you to be fully present when you rely on yourself alone. A consistent, uninterrupted focus requires a state of mind at peace within itself, not one which depends upon comparisons and opposites. The ego self relies upon inconsistency to justify its belief in both innocence and guilt. Being fully present in the Infinite Moment is, however, your natural state of awareness which is where you are now when you let go of your beliefs in sin and guilt. And that is the function of the Holy Guide within you.

The value of learning to be in the current moment is that it can teach you to be free of your self perceptions that seem to have evolved from past experiences. You must see that you have valued these experiences merely because they occurred which could not have happened if they were valueless in your belief. Experiencing being free of the effects of fearful thoughts requires that you release the value of them to see that in this moment, only the beliefs of the moment influence the experience of the moment.

Practicing staying in the moment then requires practicing unconditional acceptance. All judgments are based upon past concepts of right and wrong. The moment that is here now must be free of past events and so the thoughts that gave them birth. You do not know how to divorce yourself from your past beliefs. I can tell you this with certainty because the same was true for me as I did what you are doing. I learned to listen and give over my decisions to the Holy Spirit.

All things must serve the purpose of returning you to the truthful awareness of your Self or they serve no purpose at all. Let this be your motivation for seeking to know the only moment that truly exists and the guide God has given us will use this invitation to see that it is done.

I have a lot of pain in my back and neck, and I know it's all about grief from the past. Part of me wants to let go of this, but I also notice my very strong resistance to doing that. Do you have any insights that you would share with me about this?

The key for you most certainly is to confine yourself to the only place you truly are and that is the present. Imagine as if you had developed a case of amnesia, totally forgetting any connection you may have had to the past, bringing forward with you no memories of pain, no memories of these things that could have inflicted pain upon you. You would then have no recognition at this moment of pain or the thought that has been translated into pain as being beneficial to you in any way. And in the absence of any benefit, you would see no purpose for it. In its lack of purpose, you would not recognize it as being present and, obviously, if it is not present, it would not be in your experience.

I will call your attention again to the very simple fact that it is impossible for you to experience anything in your body that does not have its origin within your mind bank. Were you to go back and release those memories—those events of anxiety that created the pain—with the fear now having been seen as being without foundation, you would have no purpose to again mispercieve the situation and thus recreate the pain.

Returning to the scene of the crime, so to speak, has been an effective method for releasing the issues that create the pain. But in your case, I am suggesting that it would be more beneficial to simply confine your attention to right now. It has been your feeling of guilt which drives you to reexamine those past events and naturally, if you have judged yourself as guilty, then you will be guilty now. That guilt has obscured your vision of the beauty of this moment.

It will not be in the past that you will find reasons to forgive yourself. It is in the presence of your current awareness that you know your Self to be guiltless. It is here and now that you feel resonance when I suggest that you are the divinely perfect Creation of God.

Being Available

How does one be spontaneous and yet manage several things at a time without planning?

I would encourage you to think of "being in the now" as being spontaneously available to your moment to moment experiences. If you are not, you will most likely miss those things that you have already planned. Remember that those things which are now happening are the physical reflections of your thinking, showing you the meaning you have attached to them. So what is there to manage except your thoughts?

All things flow smoothly with no time restrictions when you stop resisting your Self, when you stop trying to improve the Creation of God. You have been given the perfect Planner. Spontaneously turn to It and all things will be managed perfectly.

When you are thinking, experiencing, creating beliefs, you are in a constant state of planning. And when you aren't available to the current moment because of past or future thought projections, you miss what you have gone to all that trouble to plan. When you become aware that all the planning and managing you have to do is to clearly align your focus on the *feeling* you wish to have from your experience, you will have defined the meaning it holds for you. All the details necessary to facilitate that meaning, that occurrence, will happen without any additional effort on your part. That is the nature of your experiences whether you are aware of consciously planning them or not. It is why you would deny making any unpleasant event. You do not recognize the details or specifics as being consciously planned. And indeed, you most probably did not do so consciously. But I will assure you that your perception and meaning of the experience was a direct reflection of your beliefs.

Goals and Expectations

I have been going through a transition in my life from being a very goal oriented career person to moving towards a new mission. What it really boils down to is that I don't want to do anything. I don't want more goals now. How do I handle this? Do I take my life like a puzzle and as the pieces come put them in place or should I plan for a so-called mission?

You are developing a clear awareness of the futility of goals. This has not yet become a totally integrated, conscious awareness, but it is something of which you are peripherally aware. It is this you sense that is frustrating you as you attempt to set further goals. There is a pattern that says to you that goals are quite valuable and that a person is measured by his ability to attain the goals he has set. So there is, of necessity, a conflict that arises as you, in opposition to this thinking, set a goal and after you have set it, you recognize that it was not meaningful to you. You are then faced with a choice of either saying, "I must carry out this goal which I have now determined has no value to me," or, " I must judge myself as being of lesser quality because I have been unable or unwilling to attain this goal that I have set." As you can see, both cases have been in opposition to what your Knowing is becoming.

Setting goals focuses your attention on expectation. Expectation is one of the greatest barriers to being available to the clear recognition of the experience you are having at this very instant. Expectation is a tunnel that narrows the scope through which you see the experience being available or acceptable to you. Being innocently present in every moment allows you the fullest recognition of that which you are presenting to yourself. I will also say that the fullness of the experience is always present, because every ingredient to make that experience totally fulfilling to you at the instant is present. It is only through your having not been present to receive the fullness of this experience that you do not recognize its benefit.

It will be through the process of learning to trust your Self, trust in the safety that lies within your whole Self, that will allow you to surrender more completely to the experience that you are bringing to yourself. There is also a tiny sense which you still retain which says, "Someone else, maybe God, maybe a guide, maybe some unknown entity who does not know completely what I need, is bringing this experience to me." I will reinforce to you that this is not so. You are bringing it to yourself.

When you have abandoned your ego willfulness, the need to control, and have surrendered to your whole Mind, it will be clear that this—the expression of You which is in the Mind of the Father and is in every aspect totally expressing perfection—is bringing each and every experience to you, and bringing it in a way that reflects the perfection of its origin which is the Mind of God. It will be your developing trust in that Self that will bring you the safety and the security you are seeking.

Making Decisions

Making decisions has always been hard for me, being afraid of not making the right one. Do you have anything to say about that?

There is a great confusion in the process of feeling willingness versus willfulness. The most helpful thing for you to understand as a basis for choosing willingness or willfulness is in either event you are choosing to recognize yourself. In the one case, you are reinforcing a recognition of your limited self, and in the other, you are choosing to have the trust and the faith that vault you into the unknown space of accepting a greater portion of your whole Self.

Being willful, as you have defined and currently understand the term, puts you in a space confined to experiencing only those things that you have past recognition of. I encourage your willingness to accept more unlimited answers to your questions, but not for a moment to believe that the information that you are opening yourself up to receive is coming from any other source except your greater Self. I use that term to mean a larger scope of your Self, a more whole understanding of your Self.

The difficulty you perceive in trusting that you will receive the right information is one that is derived from past experience because that experience has relied on the limited self. I am encouraging you to have faith in who you Are. I am suggesting that one of the most beautiful, experiential ways to understanding this is to open yourself up to the guidance in your day to day activities. Allow yourself to experience the far broader scope of all things that can be brought to you and the ways in which they come forth. The harmony that will be experienced will provide much encouragement to continue the process. This, of course, initially requires trust. It requires trust in who you Are. That trust is currently obtained as your ego will allow it, in small doses. But that will change as the peace you feel increases.

You begin by acknowledging that all questions will be answered by this whole Self. Understand that maybe in the beginning it will be only the little answers that you will trust and act upon. But each time you do, the experience will become a reinforcement and allow you a greater scope of acceptance for the next time you hear an answer. You will expand your comfort zone until all answers are perceived and acted upon by you from this larger scope of recognition of your Self. It is important that you at all times maintain the understanding and the recognition that these answers are coming from this expanded total Self so that you do not allow yourself to get into a space where you begin to believe, "How lucky I was," or "Wasn't it wonderful that the universe or God did this splendid thing for me." These concepts will continue to keep you from the recognition that it is you providing the answers.

There is a tendency towards a feeling of grandeur that accompanies the thought that God gave you some wonderful thing. I would encourage you to hold and own the feeling of grandeur and thereby recognize the glory of your Self. Concurrently, recognize the pleasure that it gives your Father to see you accept that which He has given you by your Creation. As you were created the perfect, unblemished, unlimited expression and fulfillment of the Mind of God, it is His pleasure to see you recognize yourself as experiencing all of that.

Security in the Unknown

In my attempt to confront my fears, I am confused about whether I'm coming from a place of being judgmental because I'm confronting my fears, or if I am being strong. Will you tell me what I'm doing?

You may rest assured that as you are pursuing a feeling of peace, if any thought is perceived as a block within that flow, you are being judgmental. You are calling up a past experience either regarding yourself or another, and paying heed to its seeming influence over your state of mind at that moment.

You will know you have found true peace when there is no thought accompanying it outside your knowledge of being totally safe and secure within a sense of Self. There will be no feeling of influence of any nature. You will see yourself as being absolute harmony. I will tell you that, ultimately, this sense of harmony will be experienced in your awareness of all other forms of Self, too. All other expressions of Self will be equally resident there. Know this is where you are headed, so to speak.

Allow yourself the feeling of being in the flow of a gentle stream, and also being aware that there is still a small root that you are holding onto that is attaching you to the bank. Please let go. Let go and recognize the stream that you are letting go into is your Self. It is the flow of your very Being. And it is only within the sanctuary of this Being, albeit forgotten by you at the moment, that you will find the security for which you have been searching. It is, indeed, a strange concept for the ego to grasp that security will be found only in the unknown, but what I will have you understand is that as you release yourself into the safety of this flow, the memory of comfort will embrace you and encompass you. You will recognize it, and it will no longer be unknown. But you will not experience it until you have made the conscious choice to open yourself to be it, and thereby recognize what it is that you are allowing yourself to flow into.

Past Lives

I have several recollections about being burned at the stake, being stoned to death and drowned, and when somebody approaches me with energy which feels similar to that kind of experience I feel extreme anxiety. How do I deal with this feeling?

I would say to you here as a point of clarification that I do not speak to you of reincarnation in *A Course In Miracles* because it would be in direct conflict with my constant encouragement to you to keep your attention in this current moment. You are aware that it is very difficult for me to communicate with you on the level of Reality in terms that are anchored within the dream. As you are dreaming, you have had a number of experiences that have been perceived as real. These you translate as having meaning by expressing them as "past lives". You see, it is your understanding that unless you have "lived" something, unless you have had a human experience of something, it must not have been real. It is in this context that you speak to yourself of lives past.

I speak to you of life present. It is not necessary for you to dwell upon what you have considered to be these past lives, nor is it necessary for you to wonder why you have produced them. It is helpful for you to understand what I have just said and that is that you now only give validity to those things that you believe you have experienced through "living" and this is why you feel it is quite important to have had past lives.

You are coming to understand more thoroughly that what is truly happening is this: Thoughts are passing in and out of a focus of your mind, a seeming dwelling of your mind in a plane where you experience physicality. And as the focus of your mind shifts between what you perceive to be an incarnate or a discarnate form of existence, you appear to have experiences that are directly relative thereto.

What we are concerning ourselves with here, however, is the understanding that this need not be. I encourage you to understand my meaning that when I say it need not be so, there is no judgment accompanying that. The information that I bring you is to allow you to make the choice to no longer experience shades or illusions of Reality, but to step beyond the veil and see your Self. I offer you the opportunity not to have a choice between different dreams, nor even to understand your dreams better, but to understand that you are within a dream now and to present you with the choice to see beyond it, to wake up. And this you do as you allow your attention to remain focused on this instant.

It is difficult for you to understand and grasp completely the true meaning of your Being as infinite when you seem to sense that it goes through cycles of beginning and ending. When you see only now, it more closely presents to you the truer picture, the truer meaning of the word "infinite." It also allows you to keep your senses completely open. I do not refer to your physical senses, but to your senses of feeling. It becomes less clear to present you with a new picture of yourself when that picture is blemished or tarnished by how you have judged yourself to be from past experiences. You try to make the concepts I present fit into the mold that you have made about yourself. What I am encouraging you to see is a picture quite different from that.

So please, let go of the "past". Let go of any prior conceptions you may have had about yourself or why you may have reacted today because of an experience you have had in the past. This will only serve to divert your focus from feeling and hearing and knowing that which is resonant with you at this instant, because it is only that which is resonant with you now that will be meaningful to you in your process of waking up. If all of the things which you have perceived to have happened to you in the past were of importance in your waking process, then ask yourself, "Why didn't they work? Why didn't I wake up then?" Let them go. Recognize it is the choices you make this moment that will allow you to see more clearly.

Although you have measured circumstances and experiences as having been either in the past or yet to come, you are reaching a point where it will become more meaningful to begin to see things as existing only in the moment in which you are experiencing them.

Now, as this may appear to be a contradiction in terms, let me say that each and every time you recall to your conscious mind the awareness of an event gone by, that "past" event takes on a current status and it is within that current status that it will be most helpful for you to allow your attention to address the issue. When you attempt to recall from the past, there is always an effort and a belief that there is something of value which occurred in the past that holds a current importance for you. I would suggest that you redirect your thinking to allow this idea to become more current. There is nothing of value to you in what you call "the past."

The Inconsistency of Separation

Why is it that even though I experience expressing and receiving love and harmony and joy as being vastly superior to any lower state of forgetfulness or ignorance, I move back into that state where I forget who I Am? Why can't I be more consistent when the difference between those two realities is so marked?

Let me first say that you have chosen an experience, which, because it separates you from others, is an experience of separation. What you are expecting is that you will completely transcend the limited aspects of the physical experience, but I will tell you this is not possible. Your choice first must be made to abandon the concept of limitation and not worry about the details of what limitation involves. Once you have decided that you no longer wish to experience limitation, you will be free of it.

You are questioning yourself based upon what you consider to be your inconsistent ability to remain in a state of peace and harmony. You do not yet recognize that peace and harmony are inconsistent with the nature of differences and separateness. You will find more peace and harmony in your life if you deal with the conflicts imposed by separateness that face you each and every day. Resist the temptation to judge yourself because the level of being able to experience the peace and harmony at any given time appears to be less than that which you desire. You are asking to be totally consistent but you are within the realm of an experience whose very nature is inconsistent. The nature of this experience is based upon what is called, "polarity." It is the experience of opposites. How, I would ask, may you take an experience of opposites and anticipate that there is any possible way that they could remain harmonious or remain consistently anything?

If there is good and bad, if there is up and down, there must consistently be a change of focus and a feeling that engenders inconsistency.

It will be the process of your being as consistently harmonious as possible as you allow yourself to be in each and every moment that will ultimately lead you to an experience of nearly consistent peace and harmony. And it will be the experience of this that will become your encouragement and acknowledgment of being able to make the choice to no longer experience limitation. I am asking you to not be so hard on yourself because it would be in that persistent act of judging yourself as being incapable that you reinforce the inconsistency that you currently find within your experience.

Whatever you are focusing upon, you must understand quite clearly, will seemingly appear more frequently in you experience. As you focus upon judging yourself for being inconsistent, that inconsistency will have a greater focus and will have a larger place within your experience. I would suggest that instead of focusing on becoming more consistent, you allow yourself to dwell more completely within that state of mind which you are calling peace and harmony. I'm sure you are aware that when you are in that state of mind, there is no recognition of opposition to it which would be perceived as being inconsistent. So why focus on the inconsistency or judge yourself when the experience seems to change? Simply allow yourself to refocus and realign your thinking to a state of mind that says, "I will be peaceful and I will experience harmony."

The Creative Present

Over the last several months I have had this recurring feeling of having a purpose and then losing that purpose or direction. It's like I'm losing my attachment to things, and I'm not sure what to do about that.

I will tell you that you are slowly coming to recognize that the purpose you had given yourself before was one which was designed to change the Creation of God, and you are now in recognition of the futility of that. As you more lovingly allow yourself to recognize your Being as the Expression of the Creation of God, you come to the recognition that it needs no change, merely your cooperation. And your cooperation is achieved in the process of giving up the illusion about yourself and simply being who you Are. This appears to be confusing to you at the moment, but as you allow yourself to relax into the firmer understanding of this, you will recognize that you have not really been confused.

The most troublesome thing about this seems to be turning down the volume on the creativeness and just being patient.

Allow me to give you an alternate way to look at your creativity. As opposed to seeing it as being a tool to change the world, see it as being the utilization of your being the Expression of All that God Is, and you are simply offering another way for you to experience it. See it as being joyful and playful, and an opportunity for you to experience your Self. You see, I am not attempting to encourage you to become a blob, but only to change or alter the intent, the purpose, which alters the meaning that you derive from the activity. The activity itself has no meaning, but only that which you give it. And as you give it the meaning of your being the Expression of God, you will see your creativity take on an entirely new dimension, one that is more joyful and freeing. And one that carries no responsibility with it.

Chapter Eight

The Physical Experience

"When your thinking has been aligned with the knowledge of who you are, that perfection is expressed in everything you experience and this obviously includes your body."

Physical Health

If your state of mind remained at all times clear of conflict, nothing would be there that would physically appear as being disease. See yourself as being a pure, clear field that we will call "energy". See the experiences, the thoughts, the creative aspects of the experiences as they flow through this clear field. If they meet with no resistance, they pass through uninhibited. When you resist them, when you build a basis of fear around them, they stop. And as they stop, you concentrate your attention upon them and as you put that attention there, you manifest the resistance as a form of disease within your body.

So how do you keep resistance from collecting in the body? You do so by being open to each and every experience with the pure knowledge that you are the Christ and there is no basis for your having fear. Your ego would dispute this based upon past experience and you would say, "Look what has happened to me in the past." I can only say to you, were you always aware of yourself as being the Christ? Have you always felt that there was no basis for fear? This has not yet been the case, and so you experience those things we have described.

The body you have is mechanical in nature. The natural body will keep itself healed and will perform the function which you gave it in your original making of it. You see, you made the body with the idea or thought in mind that it would express who you are at all times. And until you create a misperception of who you Are, that perfection performs naturally.

When you introduce the thought which creates the disturbance—the conflict within your thinking—that distortion is reflected in your body. You do not need to tamper with the original equipment; it performs quite nicely. You simply need to remove the impediments that prevent its performance and those impediments are only your thoughts. When your thinking has been aligned with the knowledge of who you Are, that perfection is expressed in everything you experience and this obviously includes your body.

Healing

When we experience disease of any kind, what is the best way for us to heal ourselves?

The body, being the mind's mirror, will always reflect the symptoms of conflict and fear within your beliefs. To speak of healing your body is to misdirect your attention and foster the belief that your body is prey to chance. The meaning this conveys to you has far greater influence on your general perception of all events and circumstances than you would currently acknowledge. It specifically and mistakenly implies that you must become protective of and reactive to your experiences and fails to recognize yourself as author of them.

It is impossible to heal the cause of your body's disease until you have acknowledged its source—your mind. It is equally impossible for a healed mind to experience physical disease.

With this understanding, the first step forward in healing your mind is to avoid judging yourself for what you could perceive as self-inflicted pain. The process of healing is one of letting go of all judgment and guilt which you have accumulated through past experiences. All disease is founded in fear. Judgments are made because you believe yourself to be vulnerable and needing protection. Relinquishing all judgment confirms that fear has no meaning because you have identified your Self as the source of safety.

There are occasions when you find yourself immersed in physical pain and feel that you are unable to be in touch with the source of fear that generates it. To linger with the pain or feel that you should endure the suffering until the fear has been discovered or its meaning made clear to you is both unnecessary and misleading. Pain would then become the price for peace and clarity, and sacrifice become a virtue. God asks not for suffering of any kind. Relieve your pain in whatever fashion feels appropriate to you at the moment. Acknowledge it is a physical curing of the symptom of fear as you honor yourself in the moment by releasing the grip of pain.

When pain is understood in this fashion, faced without judgment and released through an act of self love, you will have relieved it of all value it has held for you. Being then useless, you will require its presence no more, and you will be willing to accept a more loving reminder that your beliefs have strayed from what you desire them to be.

You will discover that the power your fear seemed to have over you, having been hidden and made inaccessible by the additional fear of the pain, is now dissipated. You are free to look upon it and, with the power of its accompanying pain now gone, see it for what it has always been; a thought brought into form with pain, a misperception made real because you see the Son of God as flesh and bone and give fear the power to punish him.

I say this to you: It will not be the medication taken or treatment applied that makes your body well. In and of themselves, they have no meaning and therefore no effect. The power any medication or treatment has is given by you through the act of loving yourself. Fear is unrecognizable in the face of forgiveness and love. A mind thus healed expresses itself in form as the physical extension of its flawless state of Being.

I am making a distinction between the curing of physical symptoms and healing of the beliefs within your mind, which are the source of your experiencing all things physical. When the body's symptoms are experienced as cured without addressing the source of fear which has made them, there has been no true healing. And for as long as the fear remains untouched, other symptoms of the same or of a similar nature will eventually appear. When true healing is misperceived, the meaning you derive from a cure is inconsistent with your real nature and is therefore of no help in your remembering of it. However, a temporary curing of physical symptoms alone is still achievable because the body does reflect the mind's thought. And when there is a clear, unfearful and unconflicted, consciously directed thought toward eliminating an illness or disease, the body will reflect that thought. I say unconflicted because if there is a concurrently held belief that the illness is appropriate, or for any reason is of value, there will be no cure.

What is the value of visualizations and or guided imagery in healing?

Any medication, treatment, or process of visualization or imagery which accompanies and clarifies the intent of the unconflicted thought thereby giving it greater power in your belief of its effectiveness, will enhance your ability to achieve the desired cure.

I call your attention again, however, to the fact that the use of any techniques you ask about can also serve you very well when your intent is to acknowledge and honor your state of Being through the expression of self love. The usefulness of the technique depends entirely on the meaning you give it.

So you see, whether you cure or heal, the guiding force remains within the meaning of your thoughts, which are always reflective of the way you feel about yourself.

Recently I experienced a healing by the use of vibrational medicine or radionics, which matches the vibration of an illness and then changes it. I am thinking about studying this process and was wondering what you might have to say about this.

There is truly but one form of medicine and that is the healing power you possess within your Self. It is the decision you make to either experience health or not to experience health and to allow your body to demonstrate that decision to you. While you are in a state of transition to this mode of thinking, you will invent many different types of crutches and they are fine. But recognize clearly that you are using these things to convince your mind to be healthy. If you are successful, they will work. If you are not, then no change will occur in the physical manifestation of the illness.

Your body is a tool of communication. One of the things it communicates most visibly are the choices you make in your mind. You see, for this to be otherwise, it would put your body in the driver's seat and in the position of control. The body, being of physical form, does not possess the infinite qualities that would be there if it were a Creation of God. The Essence of you is the Creation of God; the complete and undiluted expression of the Mind of God, and this is absolutely indestructible!

Death and the Physical Body

I don't understand why, if this is a dream, death is necessary.

In a word, it is not. Does that surprise you? It is only your acceptance of it which makes it apparently so. Should you at this moment absolutely discard the very firm belief that you hold that says, "I was born; I will die, there is a beginning; there is an end, there are transitions," you would no longer experience death. The meaning of that which you believe is transferred into those things you experience within your physical life. If there is no longer meaning to beginning and end, to birth and death, how could you possibly experience it? You see infinite life as being a process of going between the physical and discarnate state. If you saw infinite life as being a continuous flow without the need for interruption, then that would be the way you would experience it. Too simple?

If you truly had no problem with this, you would never die.

In spite of all the evidence to the contrary?

Is this the problem you have with it? Is this the problem you have as you look to have reality confirmed in the mirror of illusion? How is this so?

Well, it would be nice to have some examples of this process.

There have been many who have moved through this process in precisely this fashion I am describing. You do not see them because it is outside the scope of what you are willing to accept and believe. It is the same as looking at any other brother and believing of him what he believes of himself—that he is a limited being, and you must in some way enlighten him. You see, this is not the way it works. As you expand the scope of the limitation within which you currently operate, you will see all of the world expanded to fit those new parameters. You will see every other brother as being in a state of increased enlightenment because it will reflect that new belief which you are then in possession of.

The world does not change first and as you see it changing, you then allow yourself to change. This is merely your responding, your reacting to the illusion. It has nothing to do with the state of truth. Truth exists within your Mind, and as it becomes more apparently reflected through you, everything you see in the light of its reflection becomes more truthful. It becomes a closer perception to the Vision of God, until at last you have surrendered all illusions and misperceptions. Then you will indeed see it through the Eyes of God in its state of absolute perfection.

Perfection exists at this moment because perfection is the Will of God. It cannot change. It has never changed. It never will change. It is only your perception of it that seems to fluctuate. As your perception fluctuates, you see different depths of this truth. If you are looking to be able to see only white, and your perception currently allows you to see only black, and then you gradually allow that perception to expand until you can see varying shades of grey, your world will take on and be colored by whatever shade of black or grey that is reflective of your vision at the moment.

If there is no death, what then happens to the physical body when we leave it?

The remains of the body will be taken care of in a pattern that is in keeping with your thinking at the time you decide to leave it. Should you be at a stage where you are absolutely convinced that your desire is to take your body with you, and you know to the depths of your being that this is a choice that you are fully capable of exercising, then you may take it with you.

What would happen to it in a discarnate state?

It would conform to what was compatible with the experience you were having in the discarnate state. Your body is made up of things which appear to be extremely solid to you because, in the experience that you are now having, a solid body is the one that fulfills the purpose and function which you have chosen to have it for. When in a discarnate state, the purpose you have for a body is entirely different and, therefore, the body would conform to the purpose for which you had chosen to put it. To explain it to you in terms of its density would be misleading, for it is, in Reality, but an image in your mind.

It would be of more help to you at this point to simply understand that the body serves whatever function follows the choices that you have decided to bring into your experience. While you are in a state that we refer to as being "discarnate," your experiences are of an entirely different nature. Should you take the body with you, it would be recognized as your body, but its nature would conform to the nature of the experiences that you were choosing to have at that time.

You've been heard to say to some that this is the last time for them in physicality.

Should you choose to no longer use the state of being physical as an implementation to your waking up, then you will not experience the physical state again. This does not mean that simply because you do not choose to be in the physical state that you will automatically Awaken. Your sense of limitation is a sense that exists within your limited state of mind as opposed to being aware of Mind in its entirety. That state of mind will exist with you until you have released the limitations of it. This has nothing to do with being in or out of the physical experience.

If I choose to Awaken, my understanding is that the body is a limitation. Wouldn't I choose then to discard the body?

I cannot tell you, whether it be in this state that you exist now, or in the frame of mind that you would experience as being Awakened, what choices you would care to make at that time. I can say to you that most do find the body to be a hindrance when they are in full recognition of the limitlessness that they truly possess and they choose to have experiences which are, by its nature, more limitless. The function and purpose of the body serves primarily to identify the limits which the ego holds quite dear. Once you have gone beyond the limits of your ego, I would suggest that you would most likely not find a need to be identified as any kind of body. I would like to reiterate, however, that this in no way denies you the option of having a body at any time. To tell you that when you are fully Awakened you recognize that you have no limits, and then to tell you that you would not have a body under any circumstances, would be to impose a limit. Therefore, it must always remain a matter of choice.

Once one discards the body, so to speak, can one also recreate a body to manifest in the physical for a short period of time?

Most assuredly. Being in a state without limits allows you latitudes that you would now think to be quite extraordinary feats. But please remember that you have made your body. The manner in which you have made it does not allow you to clearly relate to the fact that you have done so in a manner which is very roundabout or indirect. So I would ask you to simply bear in mind that you did make it. Once you find yourself beyond the limits that you currently abide by, you will recognize your ability to make a body as being extremely simple.

I would call to your attention the thing that we have discussed many times, and that is the experiences that you choose to have are those which you first bring into your mind. That, you see, is the creative process; you simply decide that it will be so. At the time when you remember how Awake you really are, this process becomes more vivid. You recognize the process for being exactly what it is and you merely employ it. And that would include your desire, for whatever purpose and for whatever time, to make a body.

I would bring one other thing to your attention: as a way of illustrating to you the simplicity of what I am saying in the matter of making a body, how would you feel if I said you could as easily make a star?

Do we begin to create the body that we will inhabit before the process of birth or in the process of the fetus's growth?

Your decision as to the nature of your body is governed by your decision as to the nature of the experiences you choose to have once coming into the incarnate state. Recall, please, I told you within the discarnate state, should you have decided to take your body with you, the body would match the nature of experience that you would choose to have at that time. So as you choose the nature of the experiences you wish to have subsequent to incarnation, you are choosing the nature of the body. Because you believe in your limited ability to make the body, you will choose parents whose genes seemingly make that particular type of body most easily attainable. But that, too, is part of your dream. It is simply the way you exercise or mask the true making of the body which you had wished to have. The making of that body takes place coincidentally as you are making the experiences.

So it is an ongoing process throughout the experience we call the physical life.

What I am referring to most specifically is the general nature of your body that you have chosen to make prior to the coming into the incarnate state. It is true that once you have entered into this state, the body is continuously making changes and those changes are entirely compatible to the experiences that you are having at that time. The most dramatic evidence of this is the body changing by way of age. Because you believe as time goes by in the incarnate state that you are growing older, and because that is your belief pattern, the body obliges and does age. And because you believe in death, the body will apparently die and cease to have the function which you had originally given it. Other illustrations, of course, would be if you had chosen to manifest an illness or an accident, the body would change to fit that pattern as well. The body is an accommodation to the experience. And it serves to identify to you what consequences you have attached to the experience. As you come to a point of understanding your experiences, you will come more and more to recognize that in Reality there are no consequences, and that will be one of the reasons you will begin to wonder what the purpose of the body is truly for.

In a conversation such as this, it would be easy to think that I was putting down the body, so to speak, and I would not like you to have this impression. My encouragement is for you to enjoy the greatest aspect of every experience that you possibly can. Know the fullness of every experience. If that experience involves being in a body, then to know the fullness of it necessitates the body being present. So honor the body. Honor it for the purpose it fulfills in bringing to your conscious recognition the fullest possible aspect of the experience that you have chosen to have.

Are you saying that this step is happening because we are actually becoming more aware that we are more than a body?

You are long attempting to learn there is no creative force outside of God. Would this appearance now not seem to, at the very least, call this belief into question? In simple terms, the ego (again) is saying, "Why do you need God when you have me?" I tell you not to be concerned because I can assure you that this, as with all other attempts to deny God, will soon pass away.

Test Tube Bodies

Should mankind be trying to create a human body in a scientific laboratory? Will the Spirit of God inhabit such a body made in this fashion?

Anything which has life must be of the Spirit of God, for nothing exists outside the Creation of God. What is making this issue confusing for you is your attempt to identify the Spirit of God by the form you use to house It in and the function you would give It.

You do not need to be concerned because mankind's desire to be creative in this fashion will not be any different than its desire to create anything else. Creating a body through either intercourse or in a test tube is the same thing.

This type of activity is no different than what is already being done by the ego to recreate itself and thereby believe that it is as powerful as the God that it denies. You can't understand that what is motivating this extreme attempt by the ego to recreate itself is being brought on by its fear of annihilation. In other words, the closer the ego comes in its estimation of no longer being needed, the greater will be its desire to demonstrate that this is not true.

At what point in the development of a human form from a test tube would the Spirit of God inhabit this kind of body?

I can tell you plainly that the Spirit of God never inhabits the body and that should clarify your dilemma about abortion as well. You do not live within a body within a world. Rather, within your mind there is a thought of separation which is then experienced as a separate body within a world of different independent Beings. Within the concept of seeing the world as an experience of your thoughts, this statement should be perfectly obvious. To those who cannot accept this concept, you must wait for the Holy Spirit to find another way to reach them.

The point at which any Son of God will define itself as the (developing) body will vary to meet the needs of the perception of that one. This is why you have such a wide range of discussion as to when life enters the body.

Why would a soul choose to experience a body made in test tubes?

If you wished to experience the world of form yet again and previously, for example, had your worldly experience fearfully interrupted by your parents in a general scheme of abandonment, then this would be a most convenient way for you to avoid the experience of being "parented." But I must remind you not to attempt to make too much of this situation. I encourage you to see the similarity in all of the symbols which represent the illusion of your thinking. This is yet another of those symbols that must soon pass away.

Suicide

I have a concern about a family member who recently passed over by suicide, and I am concerned about other members of my family affected by this. Is there nothing I can do about this situation except just love?

Please understand that simply because you are unable to identify consciously the space in which he resides, nevertheless he is in the only place that is, and that is in the hands of Love. As you would welcome someone who was troubled into your home, into the love in your heart, know that this is the process that indeed takes place when one comes, as you would perceive it, to the other side of the veil. You cannot at this moment see the loving hands, and you would therefore suspect that he would be in a void floating and disconnected. Allow me to assure you that this is not the case. Could you for a moment think that the loving care that is the extension of the Father exists only in that place where you would give it recognition? You know that this is not so.

The hands which comfort him are indeed experienced in the art of love. Your desire for him to find the light is well expressed by your intention for him to find himself and the Love that he truly Is. And find it he will, as he chooses to recognize that it has always been there. I say these things to alleviate your concern, for you to understand clearly that he is in a space of resting, in a space of nurturing, and exactly where he has chosen to be.

I would encourage you not to dwell upon any negative aspect that you may hold of the suicide experience. I would further encourage you to know the same thing about the members of your family who are still on this side of the veil. Please let go of the fear. Allow yourself to be released from the fear that is attendant with every thought process which identifies you as a body form capable of suffering death and pain. Allow yourself to accept peace. Allow yourself to accept that which is most closely and truly recognized and exemplified as being a reflection of your natural Self.

The help you wish to give to others whom you feel are troubled or lost can only be extended as you recognize yourself to be the embodiment of the single thing recognizable to them, and that is the peaceful, harmonious nature of your loving Self. There will be no sense of trying to extend this feeling, for as you become more closely aligned and attuned to it, you see that it already exists in everything and everyone around you. And it is only your willingness to accept this feeling that has any meaning toward acknowledging who they are. Should I reflect to you concerns for your well-being, I would be acknowledging and reinforcing those feelings you hold which are not real. I see you as the embodiment of the Love, of the harmonious Creation that you Are, and I encourage you to see others in the same light. It will only be in your practice of doing this that you will allow yourself to see your Self.

Aging

I think I understand what you are saying about aging and death and choices and yet I don't seem to be able to stop aging at this point. Do you have any suggestions? How does that work?

The entire process that you call "waking up" is not one that occurs as you selectively make conscious choices to facilitate specific things which you feel are part of the waking up process. In this particular case, your reference is to aging and, ultimately, to death. It is within your ego thinking that could you conquer aging, could you eliminate the need for death, it would be a sign to you of progress in your path of Awakening. I would encourage you to understand that this is not true. In the same way that you do not truly cure an illness of the body by treating the body, you do not facilitate Awakening by curing things that seem to be happening to you within the dream such as aging and death.

By applying your focus to these areas, you are continuing to think of the consequences of having a body. What I would like for you to understand is that the process is one which comes from within. It comes by your continuing to feel yourself letting go of the restrictions that seem to bind you to a state of dreaming. Not to the individual dreams that are taking place, but to the general regard of the dream. It is a process of allowing yourself—not pushing yourself, not feeling that there is something for you to grasp hold of and therefore to pull yourself out of the dream—but just to be in a constant state of awareness that you are dreaming. It is a process of allowing yourself to know that it will not be forever so, and that the process of Awakening is taking place in and of itself without your conscious willing, trying, or doing. I would remind you that the state of your Being is already in existence. That, in and of itself, must tell you that any act of will which seemingly creates something is really a detriment because it is in contradiction to your already being it.

If you have chosen not to have the experience of aging and not to have the experience of death, then allow it to be so. You allow it to be so by expanding all of your other choices to go beyond whatever limits those choices seem to have accompanying them. You see, it is the total concept of either being Awake or being asleep that brings about the choices that are either obvious within the dream or obvious by being Awake.

Allow me to give you an analogy: Should you wish to buy a car, you simply decide on the color and the function, perhaps a little bit as to what the interior would look like, and then you go get the car. You don't manufacture each and every part that goes into the car. All of that is a function of what the car is. And when you are Awake, the clear reality and recognition of your choice not to age and not to experience a physical death is simply a function of the state of being Awake. It isn't a conscious choice.

All experiences of limitation ultimately bring to your attention, through experience, their lack of value. And once you give up placing value on any type of limitation, you will have a clearer recognition of who you truly are.

Senility

Why does the mind lose its short term memory as people get older?

It is not a question of the mind losing anything, nor is it a function of age or time. Your mind is ageless. However, when you accept your body as being the total identification of you, then naturally the mind is also associated with the body. And as you believe the body should deteriorate, you create the belief that the mind will follow the same pattern.

Another widely accepted belief is that you are only worthy and lovable to the degree that you can contribute to the support and pleasure of others. Since this support usually occurs in one's younger and middle years, as you age beyond your sense of usefulness, you redirect your mind's attention to that past productive period of your life. The current time period is ignored and the focus of your mind is directed away from it because you see yourself contributing no value. The only value it then holds for you is how you are able to relate it, to manipulate or reshape it, to fit into that time period when you allowed yourself to feel self value. In societies in which age is valued, equated with wisdom and usefulness, you do not find short term memory loss or senility in older people.

You ask yourself, what then can I do to change this social trend of thinking, to help older people see the value of their age and wisdom? The answer is simply this: change the way you think about yourself having to experience the aging process. If you find it difficult to accept that aging is unnecessary, try at least to discard the notion that your worth has anything at all to do with your ability or willingness to provide support or pleasure to anyone else in any way except to be consistently and unconditionally loving. It will only be in your accepting this release for yourself that you can acknowledge its validity for any other. When that acknowledgment has been wholly made, you will discover it has been forever so. There is nothing more to change.

Alzheimer's Disease

Does Alzheimer's Disease have a similar cause?

This is a form of retreat from dealing with pain when people reach a point in their life where an accumulation of fear makes them unwilling to cope with life as they are experiencing it. The pain will most often have been accumulated from a central feeling of rejection, and that rejected feeling becomes pervasive throughout their other experiences. In other words, whatever experiences they are having, because their perception has become overwhelmed with a feeling of lack of worth due to rejection, they then see all their experiences as being confirmation of this rejection.

A general feeling is developed that whatever experience is taking place would take place better without them in it, and they therefore retreat from the experience. In the beginning stages, there is a tendency to project their lack of self-esteem onto those whom they feel have rejected them, and that creates anger. The way they deal with their anger as it is experienced through the perception of dwindling self esteem, is to withdraw from that experience. The more those experiences encompass their total experience of life, the more they retreat from participation.

The body, being a reflector of the thinking process, correspondingly shuts down the neurological functions that physically characterize those activities which they are withdrawing from. Normally, these activities do not include those things which function from the automatic response system such as breathing, implementing the digestive process, or being able to spatially identify things within their vision, but it does, in most cases, shut down the response to pain which is the primary reflex that they are attempting to avoid. You could refer to it as a case of general amnesia.

A.I.D.S.

Would you address the issue of AIDS?

I would first direct your attention to other epidemics that have appeared on this planet from time to time—the Great Plague, for example. In each case, there was attendant great fear. The fear that encompasses the situation with the AIDS virus appears to be different only because of the social implications and because you see yourself being in the middle of it. There is also a feeling that this particular manifestation could, in some way, be the result of a type of social punishment.

You are able to concoct all types of punishments and will continue to do so as long as you subscribe to the belief in the concept of "sin", the concept of a Father who would see you as being a negligent child and would punish you for doing wrong. This is not the case. There is no recognition of the AIDS virus in the Mind of God as there was no recognition of the plague virus in the Mind of God.

Please do not allow the social implication or other significance which seems to have arisen around this form of plague to take on a different definition or distort your thinking that this manifestation of disease is different from any other.

AIDS, as all other manifestations of physical impairment or disease, is a reflection of inner conflict which is itself only another definition of fear. The reason it is so difficult to accept that a disease such as AIDS is manifested by your thoughts is because you translate that to mean purposefully self-inflicted. As that thought is found unacceptable, you are left with the conclusion that you are a victim of any disease. The thing you become victim to is your belief that it is possible to *be* a victim. I would say to you that any manifestation of illness is an acceptance on your part that there is room for that which is not perfect within your frame of thinking. There is a tendency to say, "That's all well and good and theoretically I can accept it, but what about the threat to our daily lives here and now?"

So I must say again, nothing will ever change in your experience unless you change the way you think about it. What you may hear as being very pretty theoretically is what I am offering to you as a very practical and "down to earth", so to speak, solution of how to eliminate the problem. Would this make AIDS disappear? As you replace your fearful thoughts with those that identify you as being the extension of the Love of God, you will not only experience personal safety, you will find it equally non-threatening to accept your brother's choices for his dream.

There is the tendency to distort or change the implication of what you see happening based upon your past judgment of the importance of it. I am encouraging you to understand that the issue that is brought to your attention in regard to any form of illness should be the one that asks you to inquire of yourself, "Am I a victim? Is there a force outside of me that can make me happy or sad, or that can destroy my physical life?" Do you truly think there is a difference between believing that there is a force that can make you sad or happy, and a force that can destroy your physical life? Because of past judgment values, you would presume the one to be a very minor infraction that you could get over by simply changing your mind and deciding to feel good, and the other having far greater implications that would be outside your control. I am simply telling you that this is not so.

Any implication you hold within your mind that there is a force outside yourself will ultimately lead you to the conclusion that there is a vengeful God. So perhaps this would be a good place to start. Instead of thinking about the enormity of the issue of AIDS, ask yourself to truly reconcile within your mind the question: is there a vengeful God? Is there a God who is capable of giving you anything except Love and the free will choice to experience whatever it is you wish to bring into your physical existence?

I am giving you an answer that is very difficult for you to accept at this moment. But I am, in truth, giving you the only answer that will ultimately allow you to come to recognize the problem you have posed.

Cancer

Why is cancer so prevalent and why has no cure been found?

It is not so much that cancer itself is more prevalent. It could be anything that expressed the ego's guilt and satisfied its need to keep its fear alive by finding threats to the body it believes it can control. This is how it justifies its fear. In the past, this looked like AIDS and the epidemic it created.

When you have experienced something such as fear for a long time, the "familiarity" of the helpless emotions serves guilt's purpose as a "painful atonement for your sins." As the thought of cancer becomes less fearful, then a cure will be found and something else will arise to take its place. To most effectively control you, fear must seem to impose a threat for which there is no defense.

The cause of every illness is the same, and so must they all have the same healing. For you to make distinctions that one has greater or lesser impact, or requires special healing, is a misperception. When I tell you that learning to Love is what heals all your misperceptions, including those of sickness, would you believe that one who has what you would call a "life threatening" type of cancer to be less willing to be loved than someone who seems to have a minor ailment or other problem?

Would you respond differently to those you perceived needed more or less love? Is it possible to love by degrees? All this confuses the limited power of the egos' ability to Love, and so to heal with that of the Holy Spirit within you. Your role in the healing process is to hold the awareness of the healing Presence now present in every mind, waiting only to be acknowledged. Only here can your faith in the power of Love be justified.

The Experience of Homosexuality

Could you give us some clarification about what the experience of homosexuality is all about?

I would suggest you not dwell on the social implications of the thing that you describe as "homosexuality". The entire concept of sex itself has been one that has been shrouded, misunderstood, misconceived, and used in many different ways within your attempt to establish acceptable social boundaries. And, as in any attempt to establish social or other boundaries, for some there will be a feeling of need to stretch those boundaries, to go beyond the limitations, to have those experiences that are not acceptable within a framework. Such is the case with homosexuality.

You see, there is always the tendency to draw great distinctions between forms of illusions. There is always the wonderful attempt to placate the ego by establishing side roads that seem to be more titillating than another, that seem to have greater or lesser significance or impact on your attempt to awaken. I have told you many times before how this is a most devious form the ego takes to keep your attention from the only issue there truly is at hand, and this is the one of knowing who you Are.

I could, on a case by case basis, give you as many technical reasons for one person choosing homosexuality as for another person not choosing homosexuality. But this again, don't you see, is simply a diversion. You will continue to validate the dream as long as you continue to distinguish things that are happening within the dream as appearing to have different implications for your coming out of the dream.

I am encouraging you to understand that what you are engaged in is the practice of the process that will change a mind pattern which will ultimately disengage an ego form of thinking. For you to press your interests upon subjects other than your own Awakening will reinforce the ego's game. And judgment is the key element that will be omnipresent. When I speak of judgment, I am speaking of it in terms that you would consider to be both helpful and unproductive, both good or bad. There can truly be no state of unconditional allowing and acceptance as long as you are in a frame of mind that encourages you to make judgments of any nature or form. When I speak of unconditional allowing, I am referring to a mind set that positions you only into the moment during which you may see only those things that concern your own Awakening.

Your attention is easily diverted from this process by a sense of need to focus on someone else's process. There are, as you perceive them, a lot of "someone elses" out there. And should you choose that diversion of focus, it could be infinite!

Soulmates

Through the years I have heard the term "cosmic soulmate" and "twin flame." Is there any validity to these terms?

From the point of reference that you are seeking this information, the answer would be no. From the broadest point of reference it is impossible for there to be anything other than soulmates that exist within the Christ. We are all reflections of one another. You are seeking to know if there are two aspects of the Christ who could be special, one to the other, and I suggest this is not an appropriate line of thinking. As there is none who is greater, it would be most inappropriate for you, in your attempt to recognize the equality and the wholeness of the Christ, to recognize that every experience that is had within the Christ is equally shared by all, and then attempt to rationalize how two of those expressions could have a special and independent relationship.

As you choose experiences which, in your mind, are chosen from a point of view which does *not* recognize the wholeness of the Mind of the Christ, you may choose to have them with special expressions who are also not in recognition of their wholeness. Those experiences will be like any other experiences of individual relationships that occur. They may transcend subsequent choices of being in a incarnate or discarnate state simply because that is the way you have chosen to have it.

Please remember, all the experiences that you are having are experiences that you carefully planned. And your plans are not limited. Should you choose to have a cosmic mate and one of you would say, "Well, I think I'll go to this end of the cosmos this time around. Why don't you go to the other and we'll meet back here and compare notes," so be it. It would be no different from your saying to one now, "I think I'll go to town. Why don't you go some where else. We'll meet at home tonight and talk it over." You are not limited in your choice of experience because each experience finds its origin within your mind. My only suggestion to you is that you do not attach a spiritually important significance to these cosmic relationships. Your relationship is based upon your choice to know yourself.

Do we sometimes come into human form with a group of friends, if you will, and touch each others lives at different times?

The answer is the same. You may have it any way you like it. You communicate and make plans with those within this carnate state. Do you think there would be some special way of not being able to communicate when you were in a discarnate state? We have spoken often that nothing changes but your mind. Being with a body or being without a body is only another choice that you make. The range of possibilities is only different based upon whether or not you chose to experience something with a physical body or not. Your mind is not resident within your body. When you have chosen to have a body you mistakenly limit your frame of reference to your mind as being that body.

When we choose to come into a physical experience, do we always stay in a human body form or do we experience a variety of physical forms here or someplace else? Do we mix things up or do we stay consistent?

The choice again would be yours. I would say to you, however, that in most cases, choices are made to experience the fullness, the maximum amount of each of what you would refer to as the "physical plane" or dimension before choosing to experience another. It is not necessarily true; it is only most often the case. If you should decide to enter upon another choice of experiences that did not entail the need for a physical body, you would be free to make those choices as well.

Why would we want to incarnate within this state of limitation at all? Why didn't I come in at another level without such limitation?

You are still operating under the impression that there is some outside influence which is "bringing you in and taking you out". Your state of mind is either limited or unlimited, or any stage in between. So wherever you "go", you do so based upon whatever your belief is at that moment. And, as you would go to any other existence, any other form of experience, because you create that experience first within your mind, you will create it either in a broader or a more narrow sense of limitation based upon what your understanding is. It's not like you're going into the discarnate state where you suddenly are totally Awake, and then say, "I think I'll dive back into this form of experience and limit my vision to this much." Your vision is always as broad as you allow it to be, but it doesn't change between incarnate and discarnate form.

Chapter Nine

Form and the Life Force

"Creation consists of a single life force. Within the physical realm, as you are now experiencing it, you do not see a unity in this life force. You see it being segmented with each of the segmented forms having a different meaning."

Defining God's Presence

When one is in the dream state of seeming to exist only on planet Earth, how does one tell what is of God and what is not regarding form, or how does one define God's physical presence within this dream state?

God, in and of Itself, is not present in the dream state. It is the recognition you have of yourself as *being* the extension of God, as *being* the expression of God, that you see and recognize within the dream because you now see a part of yourself existing within the dream. You know that you are not truly within the dream. You only seem to be. You perceive yourself as being someplace that you are not, so there is that aspect of your Self that reaches down or up, recognizes Itself and says, "Here is God." And because you perceive yourself as being "here" in another state, then in that way you bring God into your dream.

Anything that would have a sense of finiteness in any way would not be a true recognition of God. That which would have a beginning or end, or any edges, would only be your perception of what a Creation of God would be. The "form" that God takes is the form of Love. Wherever you perceive there to be love expressed in any way, you are recognizing yourself as being an expression of that Love of God and seeing it manifest. Any other form that you see is completely irrelevant; it is only the *feeling* you have for the form that is relevant, the extension of the feeling in which you recognize yourself as being the Love of God.

You could say that everything you see is God, because you are God. But that would be misleading because you have a limited perception of your Self. You are not in recognition of the Divinity of your Self, and therefore, see an illusion of the truth of your Self, and of God.

Would it be appropriate to say that those things that we experience with the physical senses are not, in their forms, the direct expression of God?

All form is a limitation. That limitation is imposed by you in the same way that you impose a sense of limitation on the Love of God. It is an attempt to package it, to bring it to the intellectual sense of knowing and to, therefore, give you some intellectual idea of what God is.

Would it be more appropriate then to say that God is the Life Force within form, but not the physical form itself?

It would be most appropriate to say that God *is* the Life Force, period.

And that Life Force is perceived by us in consciousness rather than the senses?

That Life Force is perceived in many different ways. When It is perceived in its purity, Its Essence of having no beginning and no end and as emanating nothing except Love, you are in recognition of its reality. Any other sense that you contribute to your perception of the form becomes your embellishment and, thus, a distortion of what it really is.

There is a statement in the Course that says there are not different kinds of life. The Life Force in me that is an extension of God is the same as that which is in a plant or an animal. If that is true then what differentiates a human . . .

You are beginning to create a distortion even now because you are attempting to break things down into packages. Recognize that the expression of you is the *sum total* of the Life Force of God. When you attempt to create another Life Force, you project it out into the world in a fashion that creates a difference between it and you. As that projection is made, you give it attributes that would call it a horse or a dog, a tree or a rock. But Creation consists of a single Life Force. Within the physical realm, as you are now experiencing it, you do not see a unity in this Life Force. You see it being segmented and each of the segmented forms has a different meaning. As their meaning becomes different, their form becomes different and your perception of them then becomes categorized to convince you, to confirm to you, the apparent reality of the world which is but an illusion.

If I am in this illusion because of a choice I have made, have these other life forms chosen to be separate from God as well?

There are no other life forms. There is only one true Life Form which is the expression or essence of the Creator of All. As It is indivisible, so is the Life Force. You see, if you were to believe that there were all of these other life forms that had different characteristics and traits, you would inevitably track it back to confirm your understanding that something exists outside of you. That is what is truly meant by the statement that nothing exists outside of you.

You are the Life Force that is called Creation. The experiences of Creation are many and they are varied, and as the experiences seem to be different, you then perceive them as being a separate part of the Life Force. It is when you dwell upon the need for individual identifications that you find it extremely difficult to comprehend the concept of there being but one single Life Force.

It is that within you which struggles for a need to exist, for a need to see yourself as being that which God recognizes as worthy and worthwhile, that is the very justification for your feeling a need to be individually identified. But I must say to you that in the depth of your Being, you understand quite clearly the freedom that lies within your knowing that there is no need to have a sense of being different.

I still get confused about the human experience versus a plant experience, a mineral, or an animal experience as the one Life Force.

Then you must concentrate only on understanding that there is for you but one thing, and that is your experience. Understand that when you feel a need to reach out and define what you would perceive as being a different expression of the Life Force, you are simply reinforcing your belief in a lack of continuity, that the Life Force of God, the meaning of Creation, is broken down into lesser and greater packages. You would like to think there are life forms that experience the meaning of life in ways that would be different from the way you experience the meaning of your existence. This is not so. This is but the projection of your misunderstanding. It is the basis of that thing which we call "perception". It is your projecting outside yourself a concept that reinforces your belief that something exists besides the wholeness of you.

When I speak of the totality of you, that totality encompasses all that is within the realm of Creation and that is expressed by everything you now determine to be a separate entity—a plant, a tree, another person, a cloud, a planet, a star. It is all You, in the greater sense of

You, because what is You in the greater sense is God, is Creation, is all that exists, has ever existed and ever will be. This is God. This is the universe, and this is all Love. It is only when you fail to believe that this description I have presented is enough that you begin to perceive that there are other things which you must add to it. In that attempt, you break down the Life Force into things that are more easily comprehended by your intellect, more easily comprehended by those things which are presented to you by your physical senses. It is only when you allow yourself to let go of that need that you will remember the experience of who you Are.

The information that we have made all of the forms here for our physical senses by our perception is hard for me to understand.

Any sense you have of anything being different, whether you perceive it as having form or not having form, would be your perception of, and misunderstanding of, the reality of that which is wholly God and therefore wholly You. Again, I would encourage you not to dwell upon this, but to begin from a basis of understanding which says, "I am at the center Of All That Is and there is nothing outside of me that is disconnected from me." Recognize that when you perceive this *not* to be the case, you have made another creation within the illusion. In fact, I would say that is totally how you created the illusion to begin with.

When I look out the window and see the beautiful scenery.

Concentrate on the feelings that this seeing generates within you and do not believe what your eyes are telling you. Concentrate on what your heart is leading you to understand. Your eyes would simply categorize that which you have decided is beautiful as opposed to that which you have decided is less than beautiful. Allow your eyes to be there and to share in the fullness of this experience which you have chosen. Do not deny that. But keep your attention focused on your feeling. The feeling will be the only true communicator of the message you are looking for. I would tell you it is not what you see; it is what you *feel* about what you see.

There are some words from "A Course In Miracles" about Mind which seem to be related to this. There you explain that Mind cannot make a body or abide within a body. It creates all things that are, but it cannot make the physical. (WBL 167:6) *To me, that says that all real things must be in consciousness, rather than the physical. All things of God are of that level which is not seen by the physical.*

Which is exactly what I was attempting to have you understand when I spoke to you about recognizing what you feel as you think you are seeing. It is the mind in the sense of the capital "M" Mind, if you will, that brings to you all experiences. But you then intellectualize and create a perception around them. And as you create a perception of something, you will give it form, and that form takes on a meaning. These meanings are defined by the limits of your perception. It is only when you allow yourself to expand beyond a sense of limit that perception dissolves and true meaning is understood.

If you were to have a balloon and that balloon were the representation of perception, you could blow it up and your perception would expand and expand, but it would continue to be perception because it continued to define limits or parameters within which you allowed yourself to define the experience you were having. Perception, by its very definition and nature, is limitation. But as you continue to expand the limits, it will gradually occur to you that if you blew the balloon slightly larger, it would burst and there would be no need to continue to value perception.

There is a feeling that you are protected by and find safety within that which is familiar to you. It is the boundary of your familiarity that constitutes the boundary or the limits of your perception. When you discover that your safety lies in your complete freedom, your total infinitude, you will then discover there is no need for perception. Because there is no need for safety, there is no need for boundaries. You will therefore allow yourself to expand and see completely the wholeness of every experience, and you will understand my meaning of the single Life Force being all that Is.

The One Life Force

I have read references that we have experienced life as mineral, plant and animal before becoming human beings. Is that correct?

No, that is not a true perception. Allow me to clarify it for you like this: there is but one Life Force. You may experience and understand any aspect of that energy of Life Force at any time you choose to understand it and allow yourself to be open to the experience of understanding it. You do not need to have an embodiment as being that particular type of Life Force to understand it.

Are the plant, animal and mineral Life Forces evolutionary in nature?

No, they are not. They are expressions of the Life Force that you have given perception and meaning to as being plant, animal and mineral.

I find that hard to understand.

As you see yourself being separate from other aspects of the Life Force, as you see the Life Force itself being split into different manifestations of itself, that is a perception. It is a perception that you have accepted. Since it is a perception, it is illusory. It is an illusion of the truth.

As an example, let's take my horse. Would you explain then how that Life Force is related to my Life Force?

There is, I will say again, but one Life Force. That Life Force may be seen as whole, as undivided, or it may be seen as separate segments. When it is seen as whole, it is seen in its Reality. There is no Life Force that is not an expression of the Father because the force of life *is* the expression of the Father.

So if the Life Force of a horse comes into expression as form, what happens to it when it leaves form?

The fact that it was ever perceived as being separate from the single Life Force is the illusion. It is the perception on your part that sees it out of context.

Does the human Life Force have more of the expression of the Creator than does a horse or a flower?

As you see yourself as being a separate segment of the Life Force and as you experience yourself in that capacity, then your experience will be as one who has a greater intelligence which appears to be a fuller, more complete expression of the Life Force, but that is only because you have chosen to see the Life Force as being segmented.

So it is our lack of conscious recognition of the Life Force that makes the differences seem to appear between us.

Your conscious recognition presents to you a perception that there is a difference. And if you would think about it more clearly, you would see that you also hold the perception—albeit you try not to make a distinction—you nevertheless harbor a perception that there is also a distinction between you as an expression of the Life Force and, shall I say, another more primitive human form.

Such as?

Such as an Aborigine. It is when you allow that distinction, that sense of separateness, of segmentation, to be gone from your mind that you will realize you have released another barrier of limitation.

Is it correct to perceive then that there is no difference between myself, the horse, the flower—we're all expressions the wholeness of the Creator?

You see, for you to even phrase the question in such a fashion is expressing the mistaken belief that there is a difference. There is but one Life Force. You express it. The terms within which you express it will either give it boundaries and senses of limitation, or they will not.

You have read illustrations of people who would go to great lengths of sitting before a tree in a meditative state of mind to recognize that they are the tree. The recognition that more accurately is occurring is the one that I have just described: the singularity of the Life Force that exists.

They are not the tree, they are the same Life Force as the tree.

Indeed.

Is man the most conscious of being the Life Force?

To ascribe a definition of man as being a distinctly different part of that Life Force is to confirm the misperception. All Life Force is totally conscious.

And therefore we should be able to communicate with any aspect of it.

There is no aspect of it that you are not a part of. Isn't this a wonderful barrier to remove?

Experiencing All of Creation

In a previous conversation you mentioned that I know that I have experienced every aspect of the Creation of God. If that is so, what am I doing on this little tiny planet earth, in this body with a life span of 70 to 100 years?

Let us begin by saying that your interpretation of my answer is going to be limited by your believing yourself to be limited only to that which you know and call the individual. I would like to call your attention to a question you have asked regarding whether or not I, as the individuality of Jesus, was speaking to others on the planet at this time. My answer to you then was one that encompassed an explanation as to a more comprehensive knowing of the Christ. I spoke to you then regarding a need for you to recognize that I would divorce myself from this individuality known as Jesus, and more appropriately, allow my identity to merge with the Christ, and in that capacity knowledge is being given throughout the universe.

In this context, I ask you to understand that as you begin to know yourself as not being a separate particle in the Mind of the Christ, you come to a more thorough recognition that everything that is experienced by the Christ is experienced by you because you are an integral and indivisible part of that Christ. When you think in terms of what you have experienced within the context of your interpretation as being a separate entity, you confine yourself far too much. You reinforce that it is possible for the Christ to be broken down into individual segments, but at the deepest level of your Being, you understand clearly that this is not possible. You are connected. You have never been disconnected. And it is when you allow yourself to remember this that you come to the recognition that all experiences shared by the Christ are experiences that have been yours as well.

Do not feel that there is a lack or that there would be less of a knowing in the experience itself simply because you could not identify with it as having been directly involved as an individual personality. That, too, simply leads you to the conclusion that there is a difference between you and Jesus. When I speak to you about the wholeness that exists within the Son of God, it is not a concept. It is a Reality. And as an experience is chosen by any of the infinite aspects of that Mind, it is shared by the Mind in its entirety. If this were not true, it could not, in fact, be whole. And if you do not accept your participation in each of those experiences as being actual and real, then you will never accept the fact that you are an integrated part of the whole.

It is an ego concept, a concept of separation, that says, "If I do not know it, I do not have it and it is not mine." This would constantly lead you to feel separate from every individual with whom you come in contact. You would always believe that there was an interest of theirs which did not belong to you and, therefore, you could receive no value through any experience that seemed to be taking place through the individuality of anyone else. This will also keep you in a constant state of judging the individual experiences that you see taking place and having the perception that they are experiences unrelated to you. As I tell you that you are not separate from your brother, understand that this is not an intellectual explanation. It is truth. In every aspect that you are capable of analyzing this truth, know that at any time something appears to you to be different for you than it is for someone else, then you are failing to recognize the meaning of wholeness.

I again say to you, do not feel that because I have given you this answer that it diminishes in any respect that awesome feeling that you have had as to the meaning of my original answer to you. It only takes your allowing your attention to rest in the unified Mind and you will understand that there is no experience that has been chosen by any aspect of that Mind that is not available to you as a personal experience as well. It would only be your sense of feeling limited that would not allow you to recognize the fullness and completeness of any experience as being your own, regardless of whether or not you knew specifically that it had been chosen by your individual personality.

Are you saying then that the Oneness of us is experienced in those choices we make in the illusion as well as in Reality?

You view your mind within what we call the "illusion" as being a limited aspect of your whole Mind, but do not be misled into mistakenly believing that the experiences you have chosen have simply gone away or have not actually had any value or substance. It is impossible for you to have any experience, regardless of whether you see yourself as being in a limited or a fully Awakened state, that is not available to the entirety of the Mind of the Christ. How those experiences are seen, and the meaning that is given them, will be quite different depending upon how limited you see your Mind being.

You are not diminished simply because you mistakenly believe that you are less than what you really are. It is not a case that you will have a grander experience as you allow the boundaries of your mind to become ever larger. It is only the interpretation, the seeing of the Reality of the experience, that alters as you allow your Vision to become more clear. As I say this, there will be a tendency for you then to ask, "Of all the inconsequential or mistaken choices that I have made, how indeed could they have the importance or the magnitude to be incorporated and understood within the Mind of the Christ?" And I say to you again, it is simply because you have placed a limitation and a misperception on the experience itself.

How We Created the Universe

Understand this: the Mind of God is infinite and there is no description for It. Any description that is attempted to even be placed upon It must, of necessity, form a limitation of It. This is not possible. The universes that are created by the Son of God, even one who does not recognize himself as being a part of the Mind of God, can take whatever shape and form that Son of God desires. Do not allow yourself to believe, just because you only see yourself in this moment as being a small incapable being, that this in any way limits the power of your mind.

You see, I have just told you that you have created the universe, all of the planets, the stars and the suns, and it has not registered. As you see yourself as being the Christ, as you see yourself being totally connected to the expression of the Mind of God, you would see no reason to limit anything within the Mind of God by attaching a physical form to It. It is your perception of needing to identify things, of needing to see things separate, that you currently see and experience the universe as being a disjointed series of planets and stars and suns. When you experience yourself as being the Christ, you will not have the need to see anything as being separate from, or having an identification different than, that which God has given.

I tell you this so that you may begin to lay a new foundation in your thinking that says, as I see that universe out there, it becomes my creation. As I give up my meaning, I allow God's meaning to come more clearly into focus. It is but a choice to play within a physical form within a physical universe. It is not a bad choice; it is not a good choice. It is simply a choice to play in a playground of your own making. My encouragement is simply that you begin to understand that the meaning you have given this universe and the meaning you have given the fingernail on your little finger are not the meaning of God.

Accept that you do not understand at this moment what that meaning Is, and you will allow yourself to begin the habit of being open to hearing the Voice of God as It expresses to you what this meaning truly Is.

Chapter Ten

Separation versus Wholeness

"Creation is not divided. Creation is the Mind of God and within His Mind, the concept of division does not exist. We are One. You simply see yourself as confined to a range of experiences definable by your physical senses. Please believe that this is not so."

An Invitation

I would ask you to look upon each other and recognize that what you really see, regardless of what your senses may tell you, is the Light of Christ. Be aware, as you allow your gaze to settle upon one another, that it is the same Light you recognize as being me. I encourage you to do this to bring about a better understanding that any time you look upon one another, you do indeed look upon me as well. I would encourage your understanding that it is quite impossible for this not to be so. *I will tell you this: there is nothing more you can do at this or any other moment to enhance your understanding of your Self, or to enhance the validity of your own Divinity to any greater depth, than to look upon one another and truly recognize what is there.*

Resist no thought or feeling that comes to you; it only strengthens what you resist. Resistance is based upon some past judgment you have made that something could be harmful or fearsome. So to resist means you still hold the belief that this fear is real, justifiable and worth retaining. This also means that you will continue to hold the blocks these fears have built in your mind and manifest them in your body.

These thoughts and feelings have come to offer an opportunity to choose again, an exchange program of sorts, in which continued bondage is let go for freedom. Simply access each one as it appears as to its source. Those from God will speak only of Love, for as clearly stated in the Course, "God is but Love," and, therefore, so are you. All other thoughts would hide this truth. Lovingly acknowledge they are no longer needed and choose again for freedom.

Carry no remorse or guilt that these fears were once your own. Recognize only that they are now without value to the path you are on. Don't exaggerate the act of letting them go, as that too adds importance they no longer deserve. Simply let them go. Let them merely pass through the loving light that is really you. This you can do for I am always there to help. Your release is also my own for there is no separation between us. What you do for yourself, you do also for me which takes us all a step closer to Home.

Surrender

As we have discussed many times, Creation Is. We have described Its feeling as being one of peace, and joy, and loving. When you are in a mode of resisting or sorting out, making judgments of those things that seem to be around you, then you are building a habit pattern which says that *you* need to decide which things are real and which are not. It is the changing of this pattern that is now coming to you as a feeling of wanting to surrender to all things.

I will give it to you like this: If peace is the basis for all things that exist in Reality, then how can you feel a connection with your Source unless you feel peace? What can peace be except a word unless you allow it to flow through you? I have said that you are the expression of Creation. How can you express that which you do not allow to flow through you? Creation exists. But how do you know that Creation exists unless you allow the feeling of it to be expressed through you?

All things that Are exist only as an intellectual understanding until you feel yourself to be the embodiment of, and the conduit for, their expression. And since you are the expression of Creation, all must flow through you in order to be actualized. Your experience of Creation is blocked until you open yourself to the expression of having it flow through you. What is Love except a word, unless it is expressed? And how may it be expressed unless it is expressed through you?

Creation Is. God Is. You Are. But the connection of All That Is, is blocked when you do not recognize yourself as being this conduit. I can describe it to you as the electrical system in your house: It is and exists all around you, but when the switches are in the "off" position, it does not flow; it has been resisted. Its effects cannot be apparent until the switch has been placed in the "open" position to allow the flow to be unimpeded and expressed by whatever happens to be plugged into it at the moment. To allow the actualization of what seems to lie only in a dormant, unused state, open yourself as the conduit to this flow of love and peace and harmony that is the expression of Creation.

This experience has been very difficult because it has come to you through the word "surrender," and you find it difficult to surrender to anything. So think of it as being a lack of resistance to experiencing That Which Is. What can God be if He is not expressed? And what can you be as His perfect Creation if you resist His expression by being a closed circuit? Therein lies the process of separation. It is the one of resistance. It is the process of setting up a circuit breaker that resists the natural flow of God as He is being expressed through you.

You may wonder at this moment how important it could be to not resist many of the things that seem to flow through you while you are in a state of being unrealized, of seeing yourself as being a shadow of what you truly are, of what we have referred to as being an illusion of truth. But don't you see? That *is* the illusion! The illusion is that there has been a circuit breaker placed between the truth of God and what you seem to be experiencing.

You keep expecting that if you were to be out of the illusion, you will drift out into another realm somewhere. There is no other place for you to go. There is no other way for you to be. You will not become a different person. You will only recognize the actualized person that you have always been and this actualization process takes place when you open that circuit breaker and allow the flow that is God to be unimpeded, to be naturally expressed, as you are only the natural expression of His Flow.

That is why it is coming to you in terms of "surrender". It is your Being that is encouraging you to give up resistance. And the way that is best seen now is for you to give up resistance to everything. Please hear me when I tell you that as you allow this process to take place, as you give up resistance to all thoughts and activities occurring to and around you, those things which seem to be taking place will begin to have a different appearance. Their appearance will change because you will discover that as you no longer resist them, you will give up judgment of them. You will just allow all that is happening to run its course. In that way, you will be encouraging yourself to be equally open to the flow of this more Real World to become apparent. As your judgments are lifted, your fears will dissipate. You will see the evidence of your total safety.

How does choice become experienced within this flow of non-resistance? Do we still make choices?

The expression of Peace and Love, which are the expression of Creation, has as many possibilities as does the expression of an illusion. Your choices when you are in a realized frame of Mind constitute the movement of Creation. But the movement is seen differently as your knowing of Creation is expressed in its true and natural form. As choices are now made to express chaos and conflict, choices are then made to express peace and Love. That is the movement of Creation. That is your allowing yourself to move within the framework that expresses God. You will recognize your Being as the expression of God, and you will recognize what you now call choices as being the expression of Creation, that which is called, the "Will of God". You will recognize that this is also your will as you see yourself being the vehicle for the expression of God. God exists. He Is. He is the basis for all Creation. But His Creation cannot be expressed until you allow its expression to take place through your Self as the vehicle which God Himself put in place to illustrate its movement. That vehicle is you! *You are the movement of Creation.* And when your choices are made understanding *only* this, you will see Creation through the eyes of God because you will recognize your Self as being those eyes.

See it like this: If all of Creation, everything that was the Creation of God could be represented by your car, what would the purpose for the car be without its driver, without its mover? And that is you! Please do not have the illusion that this car does not move unless it is moved by you as you see yourself in this limited state which you now consider to be yourself. Creation has not been static; it has not had a lack of movement simply because you have not seen yourself as being in the driver's seat. You have *always* been the movement of Creation, but you do not recognize that this is what you have been truly doing. Your function and your purpose have not changed. What you have been doing as the expression of the Creation of God has not stopped; it has not changed. You have simply mistakenly believed yourself as being disconnected from It.

The flow of Creation already is. The appropriate thing to do is to allow yourself to simply be aware of Its movement. I have also said that You, being the wholly unified and infinite Son of God, are the only movement of Creation. And the two are the same. When you do not see them as being the same, you are seeing an illusion of your Self. You are seeing an aspect of yourself that is removed from truth.

So as you allow yourself to become a conductor or conduit of the flow of Creation, as you stop resisting this knowing that is building within you, as you experience the natural flow of your Self, you will remember your Self. It will be in the act of doing that which is so natural for you that your memory will return.

Being in a state of total non-resistance is helpful, even if it is in non-resistance to your dreaming, because it will be this acceptance that will help you to recognize your natural feelings. It will be in your acquiescing to all things, including the dreaming, that you will allow yourself to give up the dreaming. Please remember what we have said. The importance lies not in *what* you are doing, but in *why* you are doing it. So as you feel yourself being non-resistant, you will recognize that the reason you are doing it is because it is reflective of who you Are. It is reflective of your being non-resistant to being the flow of God, to being the unrestricted expression of Creation . . . of seeing yourself as bringing God into actualization.

There is no meaning to God unless He is expressed. You are that now. It is happening now. And in allowing yourself to be nonresistive to all feelings, you will be not be resistive to this one as well. That is what I mean when I say, feel yourself being in the flow and recognize that the flow is who you Are.

This then, also answers your question of what is your purpose. Your purpose is simply to recognize that which you already Are, which is the expression of God.

Releasing the Sense of Separation

How does one overcome the sense of separation to experience Oneness?

The recognition of your Being occurs as you recognize my Being, as you recognize the Being of every brother as an extension of your Self. As you approach each circumstance that comes to you and you think you see that circumstance as having occurred in another space outside your own, you seem to recognize separateness.

There have been many attempts to explain the "mirror principle." Most have not been clearly understood. What you frequently believe you see in others are their problems and then you interpret the mirror principle to mean that because you see these problems in them, they really exist with yourself. While this is true, and the knowing of it encourages you to be less judgmental of others, it also focuses your attention on the negative issue of problems as opposed to the positive choice of peace. And it provides additional negative opportunities to judge yourself in the light of your perceived shortcomings. While your ego would be delighted to suggest that you should see your brother with the same misperceptions you have of yourself and would claim that this is an appropriate sense of your "oneness," it would only be a confirmation that your dream was real.

What has truly been asked of you in using this concept is not to see what is reflecting on the surface, but to see in them the *perfection* that exists beyond the mirror, and to recognize that as being your perfection as well.

To more specifically address your question of how to overcome any sense of separation, it would be helpful for you to see this perfection not as being identical to your own, but to see it as being your own which acknowledges the Source as being totally whole. The sense of individuality which you now perceive as personality is one that tends to enhance the feeling of separation. Individuality, more appropriately, deals with the continuing unfolding of the Mind of God in a multitude of loving expressions.

What we are dealing with is an attempt to recognize the Reality of you that exists beyond what you would term the "dimension" that you are currently in, and even another dimension that you are apparently striving to achieve. This can be made far more simple by your understanding that what are referred to as "dimensions" really are only differences in your state of mind. The connotation of dimensions brings forth a feeling of some place else to be, and that concept, in turn, presents to you a feeling or a need to achieve, of something to be done, a way to enhance yourself in order to make a transition. This necessarily results in confusion. What I am suggesting to you here is that everything that exists, everything that you see, exists and is seen by the state of mind that you are currently experiencing. To experience differently involves only a change of your mind.

There is no distance between what is described as the "third and fourth dimensions." There is only a different way of thinking. Where could you go when you are already in Paradise? The Kingdom of Heaven is not a place. *The Kingdom of Heaven is simply a state of Mind that recognizes the unity and harmony of the Mind of God.* The recognition of your brother is resident there.

How do you achieve this? It is a state of Mind. Because you are accustomed to working with patterns that establish habits of thinking, this is done by changing your habits, changing your mode of thinking about each new experience. Every contact you make, be it with a bird, a brother, a tree, or a blade of grass, is an opportunity for you to experience your Self by seeing differently, by seeing beyond the distortion of physical limits and by allowing your natural state of Knowing to be your interpreter. It is always present, continuously, if not consciously. Therefore, what we are after is a mind pattern that encourages this recognition and establishes new habits of thinking.

Take each and every opportunity to see wholeness, to see the harmony of your Being which is constantly trying to get your attention. You may find this much easier to do when you hold me in your thoughts. There is a representation that I have for some of you that allows the clarity of a perception of perfection. I can assure you that I present myself to you with every contact of a brother that you make. Allow your new patterns of thinking to reinforce this realization. Know on a very personal basis that there is no difference between you and me. Be equally aware that there is no distinction or difference between you and me and any other. The practice becomes one of recognizing this simple truth.

Trust and believe that the Love of our Creator is not withheld from, nor in any way changed, in any Son within His Mind. The reminder has always been that there is but one Son of God. There are an infinite number of expressions of the Son, but there is only one Son. How then could even the rational mind perceive this wholeness to be in any way different, one from the other?

The allowing of a sense of difference based on a behavior which you see occurring within a dream reinforces the feeling that there is a difference between you and any other brother. Seeing beyond this is seeing within your Self, seeing that which exists in Reality.

The Feeling of Joining

In the beginning of a sharing together, Jesus tells us of his very real Presence with us.

I would encourage you to recognize that, on the broader level of your Being, this is what is known as communion. Please know that I am with you now as fully and totally as you experience each other. I want you to know this and become comfortable and accustomed to this feeling. *Know that it is one you may have at any time with any brother, be he incarnate or discarnate.* Become one with this feeling that you may know there is no real difference between the birth and death sides of perception.

Creation is not divided. Creation is the Mind of God, and within His Mind, the concept of division does not exist. We are one. You mistakenly simply see yourself as confined to a range of experiences definable by your physical senses. Please believe that this is not so. It is only your state of mind that confines you. Our joining is as real as if I reached out my hand and touched you.

Would you like to direct the conversation with us?

It was my intent that the feeling we are generating together would be the path. I'm sure you are aware that this feeling of being joined, not separate from one another, allows you to begin to have a true perception of the total Self you are reaching for. As you open more to this sensation, your feeling will encompass even wider boundaries. And though they still remain as boundaries, they are expanding.

This is the feeling that brings you into greater contact with your Self as an expanded, cohesive, whole Mind. At this moment it is much as if you were blowing up a balloon. As you feel the expansion of the balloon, you are aware that it still is confined. Nevertheless, you see the expansion and are aware that you may apply the pin which will burst the balloon at any time you choose and remove all of the boundaries.

You see, when you have been concentrating upon yourself as a body, and you then recognize yourself expanding beyond your body, you assume there must be some other limit that you are going to expand into. I would describe this as the basis for the fear of truly letting go because you do not know what you are letting or allowing yourself to expand into. You have become so accustomed to boundaries and limitations that it seems only natural that even in your expression or feeling of infinity, there must be some type of boundary around infinity. So what are you going to allow yourself to expand into? How far can you go?

Think about it like this: Hold a thought in your mind of anything you choose. Recognize that it is a thought, that it is your thought, and that this thought can change and expand. It can take on a different form or no form and, as you allow yourself to flow freely with it, you begin to discover that there need be no boundaries at all around it. Remember, it is your own thought. Are you not comfortable with it? Is there fear associated with it as you recognize it to be limitless, without boundaries, infinite?

What I am encouraging you to understand is that as you allow yourself to be in what I will describe as a limitless state of Mind, that is You. You are what you expand into. That is precisely what happens when you allow yourself to prick the balloon and set your Self free. When your thoughts become as free as your thoughts have always been free, you do not confine them to any limitation or association with a boundary regarding your physical body. You are as free and as limitless as you allow your thoughts to be.

As the fear of the unknown comes into your mind, be aware that there really is no such thing as the "unknown". Each limitation or boundary of your mind that you allow yourself to remove reveals the answers you have been seeking. Everything you had considered to be unknown and fearful now becomes revealed and familiar. In terms that you would be more comfortable with at this moment, I would simply say, think about what you want to know and understand that there is only a veil in your mind that stands between you and your knowing of it. When you choose to release fear, you push back the partitions within your mind that seem to create a concept that there is a known and an unknown.

You are It, my wonderful brothers. You and I, we are It! There is nothing more to be known beyond what you Are. And I would remind you of something that you already know; what you are is Love. It will ultimately be love that will release your fears and your sense of boundaries. It is a feeling of love that knows nothing but trust, complete trust. And that trust has its basis, its very foundation and its wholeness, in your knowledge of who you Are. You have a sense that I know this, so embrace me. Embrace me and know your Self, for I am you and you are me and together we are the undivided reflection of our Father. This is all you really want to remember.

You recognize this truth, but part of you asks, "What does this have to do with dealing with the problems of my daily life?" And dear ones, the only way I can respond to you is to say that the problems you perceive as being in your daily life are only there because you do not sit in this place of peace and know who you Are!

There always appears to be something to do to bring yourself to this state of knowing your Divinity, but I have suggested as we began to commune earlier, that we allow ourselves to be joined and to feel the peace that is present in our joining. The peace has not been created by our joining; peace is what and who we Are. It is simply experienced because we have chosen to experience the joining. You have chosen to be in this experience. You have chosen to have the problems that you seem to be having. You may choose not to have them. You may choose to recognize your Being. You may choose to recognize that it is a state of endless harmony.

When someone brings a problem to me and says, "Please help with this," in truth, the only help that I am able to give is, in one way or another, in whatever language is understood by that person at that moment, to say to them, "You don't need that problem; you are not that problem. You may choose not to experience that problem." There seems to be a constant feeling that as you alter your problems, or "solve them", as you say, you will come into closer contact with your Divinity. My advice more truly would be give up the notion of problems.

Do we do this by moving into that space of trust?

Indeed, it is that space of trust, of recognition, of remembering your Self. When you can grasp that feeling of who you Are, you will experience absolute perfection. It is Divinity. It is God. What can you do to improve upon God? What answer do you seek that does not lie in simply giving up the illusion of the question?

Some have perceived of me that I lived my physical life perfectly. I can assure you that it was not quite as perfect as I would have, at the time, liked it to be. There were many moments when I felt drawn away, many moments when I was drawn away.

When you were drawn away, do you mean into your ego?

By my description to you of an "ego", I most certainly was. I am trying to express the difficulty that does exist within this plane of limitation, this human experience.

Then being Awakened is not a permanent state? Can an Awakened Being oscillate, dance back and forth across the line?

Rather than my trying to answer your definition of being fully Awakened, let me give you mine in the hope that our communication will be more clear. A fully Awakened Being is one who sees no line upon which to dance. A fully Awakened Being would not choose to experience the limitations of the physical realm. There is simply no need for it. What I was referring to when I spoke of my own "dancing", as you have put it, was the dancing that I experienced while in the physical form. My dancing now is of a different nature. The tune I hear is one of perfect harmony. It is the same tune you hear but do not frequently acknowledge.

How Close Are You to God?

How close are you to your next breath, your next heartbeat? I use these as examples because at this moment they are representative to you of what keeps you going, what seems to represent life itself. More appropriately, I will ask how close are you to the Spirit Essence that actually does constitute the wholeness of who you Are?

Please slow down and focus now very clearly on the feeling that the meaning of my words will convey. The Essence of Spirit is the Thought of God. It is the way He chooses to express Himself as the very nature of Creation. It is the way He has chosen to see Himself. And it is you! This is what I have been telling you when I have said that you are the very expression of all of Creation—the whole expression of its Creator—the only expression of God.

The Mind that moves All That Is is the force of uncompromising, unconditional Love, which constitutes the makeup of your Being. Its identity is inseparable from yours. Don't allow yourself to be overwhelmed by this thought, or you will have the tendency to diminish its significance and reduce yourself to proportions more easily acceptable to your ego.

Now, let's return to your question. How close are you to God? How completely are you willing to accept what I have just reminded you of? Again, please be very attentive, because your response will actually be the description of what constitutes the nature of illusion. What I have told you is truth. Your lack of willingness at this very moment to acknowledge it is the total substance of your illusion.

The answer to your question is that you are as close to God as your willingness to let go of the thought, the misconception, that you ever had the option or ability to change or alter in any way what I might call your natural birth and infinite state of Being in the Mind of God. Let this be your celebration of the birth of the Christ within you. Express your joy by allowing the nature of your Being to become transparent, by extending and experiencing the flow of Love which is God—and you.

Thoughts of One are Shared by All

There is still felt by many a factor of limit, a feeling that would tell you that in some way you are here together as pockets of expression of separate individualities. And what I would like to share with you is the magnitude of limitation that this thought would keep you in. As we are together this moment and share ourselves, it is a sharing that has no limit. It is felt quite literally by all of consciousness, by the entirety of the Mind of God. I would invite you to open yourself to this feeling—it will indeed help you to know the breadth and scope of who you truly are.

As you feel the peace and love flow through you, know that it touches every sense of consciousness in Creation. Know that you are in no way disconnected. You are not a small particle of that consciousness, but the possessor of the totality of it. You see, there is no flow that does not touch you, that does not encompass you in every way.

I have spoken to you of this flow as being a stream that has no beginning and no ending and which feels no difference within itself. It does not know itself drop by drop; it naturally feels its wholeness. I would encourage you to feel and to know that about the Essence of your Self. There is no boundary to You, there is nothing that closes you off, or separates you from the entirety of the Mind of God except as you would feel that boundary existing in your mind. I invite you to join the entirety of the stream, to feel yourself connected to Everything That Is, without exception, without a feeling of needing to know how or why this can take place, or worrying in any way about the mechanical aspects of how this is happening. Simply know that it Is.

It will be in your acceptance of this very simple truth that you will allow yourself to experience it as it presents itself to you in words and feelings, even in sights and sounds. What I am asking you to experience is the Infinity of your Being.

This flow of consciousness is the stream of feeling, of energy, of Love that we are all a part of and immersed in and identified as. Please allow yourself to be in this space. Please accept this recognition of yourself. Know that I, as you identify me, am here merely to facilitate your recognition of your Self. Build no barrier between what you identify as your Self and me. There is none. We are together the consciousness of Christ. There is no way for any one of us to be separate from that, so please feel our joining. Allow that which we all share in common—which is the Essence of us—to be recognized and felt, to be shared with joy and great rejoicing that in this recognition of us, we bear the Presence of our Father.

Teaching Others

The Course states in many ways that you want us to teach the thought system that you share in the Course to others. Will you give me more insight on the teaching aspect you've given us in this material?

I have said many times in *A Course in Miracles* that you will teach what it is that you have chosen to learn. And in this regard, your teaching of anything becomes valuable to you. I suggest that the value will be diminished as you hold an expectation as to what that teaching will mean to someone else.

Perception is a very personal thing. Each individual's perception is comprised of the patterns and the ego filters through which they have seen the world based upon experiences they have chosen in the past. This will allow you to see truth only as it is applicable to you and as it is fed through those filters. It is unlikely that anyone else will have had the exact experiences, or will have constructed their filters in the same fashion in which you have and, therefore, their perception will be quite different. It is for this reason that it is impossible for you to teach anyone else anything at all.

As you engage in the process which we have identified in *A Course in Miracles* as "teaching", you are selecting those things that you wish to bring to your own attention, and it is through this process that you allow yourself to have the experience. As you engage in the process, your awareness expands. Your awareness of who you Are becomes clearer to you and as this happens, you offer a unique opportunity to those around you. Their opportunity becomes one of seeing who they are as they look into your eyes and see reflected there your clear knowledge of who you Are. But you must only view this as an opportunity you merely offer. Attach no expectation to it. You must allow them the choice to either see or not to see. For you to do less or attempt to do more, would be to make a judgment that God Himself has not made.

As He has given you the freedom to choose whatever it is you wish to see, you must do the same for those around you. Do not stand in judgment because you perceive some to be less than what you have determined they should be. I will tell you of a certainty, this will be of no help to them and it will be less than helpful to you because every failed expectation will seem to be a step in the wrong direction. This is not true in Reality, of course. But in the perception you hold of yourself, it appears to be true.

You exist at this moment in the unchangeable state of perfection. It is in this state that you are clearly seen by your Father. What I am suggesting to you is a process that will allow you to let go of any current notions or misperceptions about yourself so that you may see yourself and those around you in the same way.

I have said in *A Course in Miracles* that you are in a state of illusion. I use this word because it illustrates most graphically that you see yourself differently than you are seen by God. Truth is only seen through the eyes of God. When you do not look through these eyes, you will not see truth but only an illusion of truth. When you see your brother as needing changing, you will be seeing an illusion of who he is, just as you see an illusion of who you are. So as you attempt to engage in a process that says, "I will change him," you are only strengthening the illusion of how you already see him and you are teaching nothing to him or to yourself.

There is but one thing for you to do. And that is to let go of the misperception of who you Are. When you look through the eyes of your natural Being, you will discover they are the eyes of God, and you will not see a flawed brother. And you will not see yourself as less than the perfection in which God created you.

I would also like to explain this to you: the nature of God, the pattern in the Reality of all of Creation, is one of harmony, love and perfection. But that pattern exists only as an idea until it is experienced. And it is through you that this experience takes place. It is when you are in a state of understanding who you Are that the entire meaning of Creation becomes expressed. It becomes expressed because it has been *experienced.* That is why I say there is only one thing for you to do: know your Self. And in that knowing you will experience, and in that experience you will express, and what you will express is God and what God Is which is Love. What you will see then will be only Love, because you will only see what you can express, and you will only express what you can see. In the dream, you express a state of limitation because that is what you see; it is not what you Are. So I suggest that you change your vision. Let go of the misconceptions that you hold about yourself. Many times in your life you have heard in your mind, "Surrender to God." This is the meaning of that phrase: surrender to God's identification of You. Know your Self, and you will express God.

Now, I will also tell you one other thing. You are at this moment already doing precisely what I have described, but you are not doing it in a way that you recognize, and that is why I say that you are having a dream. You are having a dream about doing something else. Therefore, you see a misperception of yourself; you see your functioning in the dream as being real and therefore you do not see yourself as expressing God. And so I have used the term, "Wake up!"

Wake up to understand that you have always been the expression of God, that you have always lived in a state of absolute harmony. Do not attempt to involve your intellect in an understanding of how something could appear to be so real and yet be called by me merely a "dream".

There will be no understanding for it. And do not resist it, do not try to get out of it, do not think that by dying you will go from one plane to another. There is no place for you to go. You are now at Home. You have always been at Home, and it will only be when you allow that recognition to dawn upon your mind that you will see it as being so. You will see the glory of God that has always been around you. You will see the state of Love that you have always been in. But you will not see it if you either resist it or try to make it so. Just give up the belief that it is not so.

There is nothing else to do.

Summary

The Holy Experience

"There is no right way or wrong way. There is a way that conveys a message of Love, and there appears to be a multitude of others."

The Holy Experience

It is always my intention to share with you all that I truly Am, to ask you to join with me in recognizing that we are the Love of our Father, and then to demonstrate the wholeness of all through our unity with everyone. In that light, what else would it possibly be that I would bring to you?

I would ask you this: What would it be that would reveal the key to your recognizing and remembering the Divine wholeness of your true Self? What words of wisdom would you seek that would make this known to you? What "Holy Word" could I offer you in this moment which you could forever cling to that would suddenly and magically return you to your right Mind? What words have I been offering for what you would perceive to be these last two thousand years?

I see that each of you would have your own opinion of this. Each of you would present a different definition of the most "Holy" word. Each of you would bring a different feeling to bear about the significance of the holy word that you had perceived as being the expression of God. So then, have the holy words offered these two thousand years changed so much? Or has the *meaning* been lost by your attention dwelling only upon the holy words themselves?

I have said to you in many ways and at many different times that to recognize yourself as being the Holy expression of All that God Is is the only significant purpose you have. So where has this become lost? Where has the meaning changed? Why do you now see that holy word as being so different? Could it possibly be that the "Holy word" has gotten in the way of the Holy feeling?

Could it possibly be because you cling to the idea of being separate from your brothers so tightly that you would use the Holy word to validate that you were right and your brother was wrong? How Holy has the word become when you would turn its purpose to this intent?

If there is but a single thing that stands between you and the recognition of who you truly Are, and that single thing is your acceptance of the wholeness of your Being existing as an expression of the Loving Mind of God, then how is it possible you would remember this by denial of your brother in any way?

Were you to see these two thousand years as something you might describe as a "time warp", you would see the pattern of conflicting beliefs now present being no different than that which existed then. You would see each brother struggling to be right, as he was determined to prove that his comprehension of the word was more Holy than that of another.

So I offer you a choice; a choice to end this conflict, a choice to see that it is not what your brother says, but to know that it is the Love he represents that defines his Being, that defines your Being. And it will be that recognition, *and only that recognition*, that will close the gap that seems to exist between you.

On the lighter side, I will say this to you. Even if your choice is to continue to believe in the differences that would apparently exist, do not be disheartened because you will not change Reality. You cannot drive your brother further away simply because you choose to ignore the connection that exists between the two of you. You cannot undo what God has done, nor can you make right what you have apparently done. But you may choose at any moment to simply let the illusion go and accept what Is, accept what always has been. I will further suggest that you may make this choice at any moment, and the moment that you choose will not be charged with time. It is not incumbent upon you to Awaken this moment if you choose not to.

There is a question in your mind as I say this, because you hear much about the relevancy of time as it pertains to your Awakening. I am suggesting to you a gentler approach. Time is not a product of God; it is not of His making, but of yours. As you would transpose the belief that time was imposed upon you by God, you can very easily convince yourself to feel quite guilty about not waking up right now. And with that belief, you would have automatically reconfirmed to yourself you were asleep when, in fact, you are not. You are at this moment perfectly Awake, fully expressing the wholeness of All that God Is, but you do not acknowledge this to be so.

Your dream is of your making. God does not see your dream, nor will He impose upon you a belief that it is real by encouraging you to abandon it at a moment of His choosing. As time does not exist in Reality, the moment you thought you went to sleep and the moment that you must choose to Awaken will be the same moment.

The process that you are engaged in now is one of remembering your Self as being an expression of Love. As you would bring to this process activities and ideas that would not be in concert with that basic principle, you would be at odds with what you are trying to do. And I will tell you that your belief in time and the pressure it would seem to impose upon you is contradictory to your very nature. This thought is not pleasing to an ego whose demand it is to change the world, to change that which is seen outwardly while ignoring the very cause in your own mind.

Are you so sure this moment how your world would appear to you to be if you saw it wholly and only through the eyes of the Loving God? As you would heal your physical body by allowing your mind to become whole, what might you suppose would heal your ozone layer? What might you suppose would heal the rain forest and all of those things that seem to be victim to an angry and savage world? Are you so sure what the cure for these things must be? Are you so sure that the healing of your body is so different from the healing of any other aspect of the physical world you see around you? I have said to you many times that it is impossible for you in any way to become a victim of the world. How then, is it possible for the world to become a victim of you? By that kind of reasoning, this world that you see being damaged and being torn apart by you would surely then be your victim.

But what could you seek to heal that would not be healed by your acceptance of your Holy Mind? What would not reflect the Loving Creation of God were you able to see it through His eyes? Or perhaps you do think it is possible that you have indeed changed the reality of God, forever altering His Creation to what you now see? As surely as you would believe it is possible for you to destroy your body, and thereby destroy the creation of what you might believe is of God, then you would see the world around you reacting in that same way.

The Who of you, the Reality of you as it exists in the Mind of God, is no different from the Reality of any other aspect of Creation which you have given misidentification to. And the healing of each of those things has but one common source: the healing of your mind. It will be the healing of your perception that will correct the way you see the world. What meaning do you bring to your recognition of who you think you are as you would struggle to save the environment you see around you and ignore the environment that exists within? The "world" of God does not need saving. Its Creation lies forever safe and secure. What purpose then brings your recognition of this but to heal your mind?

As I say to you, "I bring all that I am to your Presence, and all that I am is the loving Thought of God," what words of wisdom will convey this message to you? This is who you Are. This is everything you Are! And all the wisdom that you seek will bring no meaning until you allow it to be embraced by the *knowing* of this.

All differences your brother would seem to present to you will but acknowledge a mistaken belief that you are separate from the Mind of God if you see them as bearing any other meaning than that he, too, is only the loving expression that you Are. I ask you to consider becoming joined, recognizing the wholeness that now exists between you and All That Is. I would suggest this would begin by knowing that the brother who walks next to you bears all the love and the wisdom you have ascribed to me. And I will say this to you if that one appears to offer contradiction to every thing you hear me say.

When you referred to the ozone layer and the environment being healed, am I correct in understanding that as we individually heal our mind, the reflection of that then heals the planet and there is nothing that we need do except be the expression of Love that we are?

I say to you *unequivocally*, the absolute truth of the principle that I present is simply this: the world you see as being expressed around you is but a reflection of the world you see within. As you would see anything outside of you torn asunder, you must recognize it is your belief within that you are not whole. On the other hand, as you would see your whole Mind being indestructible in its natural state, as being a reflection of the perfect Creation of God, you will see that perfect Creation portrayed flawlessly in every experience you choose. I say to you again and again, the world that apparently exists independently outside of you *is not so!* It is but a reflection of what you see within.

Since I have said to you that God does not share in your illusion, does not see you being in a state incongruent with knowing only that which is the expression of Love—could I then tell you that your healed mind would view your physical universe in a fashion less than this? I would encourage you to adopt the Vision of God. Should you choose to do so, what then would happen to the environment that you now see and experience as being in the physical world outside of you?

The world of God exists as the expression of You. As you would appear to express that outside yourself in the creation you have made, you will see it in whatever form of trueness or distortion that you have adopted as your belief of who you are. As you allow the distortion to go away, and you now see the real world, the Creation of God as it exists within His Mind, you will see it existing in a state of perfection because that will be your natural state. This seems to be a principle that defies all of the logical input that your intellect may accept about it, but that does not change the truth of it.

I could also say to you that your world exists as a direct reflection of what you believe about God. It is the same as saying it exists as a reflection of what you believe about yourself. And as you see either reflection being in a state of less than perfection, you will experience the chaos and the turmoil and the conflict that your belief would reflect back to you.

You have the feeling that it is too simple this way; that you must be missing some meaning, that I must give you some other definition of cause and effect in order to make this possible. But I have given you the truth of it. You need but to allow the idea of the complexity to disappear to see the Reality of it. Ask yourself if it is possible for that which God has created to be perishable. You know it is not. So as you would seem to see the world in a state of decay, what is the cause? Is it decaying because it was designed to decay? Or is it a victim of your perception?

Now, as I have said all of this, am I asking you to ignore what you see happening in the world, to ignore the world that appears to be decaying around you? Indeed, I am not. But I am saying to you there is a different way to heal it. There is only one way to heal it. If you would continue to deal with changing the effects, you will find yourself consistently experiencing disappointment and frustration because you may only rearrange the effect. To deal with the cause, you must get to its source. The source of all Creation is God, and the expression of all Creation is You. And as you recognize that the source exists in a state of perfection, you have but to allow the expression of that perfection which is You, to acknowledge that this is so.

Would it be helpful for us to gather together and, while focusing on being the expression of love, send love to the environment that seems to be in danger?

It is not the environment that requires the sending of your love. You persist in seeing the need to project something outside yourself to effect a healing, but I am saying to you the only healing that need occur is that which exists *within your own vision* to the extent it appears to be less than the Vision of God. Send nothing into the environment but a reflection of who you Are and you will see it existing in a state of wondrous perfection. You do not need to project it there, you need to simply see from within and you will recognize that it has always been so.

If the environment, as you see it, were really one of God's precious possessions, would He not prevent you from ruining it? Were it to truly be in danger, would He not step in to prevent this from occurring? Were you to be in danger because you do not see who you Are, would He not step in to prohibit this from happening? What I am giving you is the definition of your illusion about yourself. You cannot change the Creation of God. You cannot mar its beauty. You cannot tarnish your own Divinity—you can simply accept to see it, or not. And time plays no part in this.

Were you truly to accept what I have said, would that not lighten your burden? Could you not then accept your expression of life as being a joyful one?

How do we accomplish this healing?

Allow that which is not true to have no meaning for you. It is a process of allowing truth, which is pre-existent, to be recognized by giving up the illusion of that which is not true. You are seeking a magic formula of what to do, of rules set down from one to ten that you could follow each morning and each evening. And I will say to you that although there is a time when this may be a help, as you become attached to the belief that it is the rules that are allowing you to Awaken, you become convinced that you have all this time been asleep and that the illusion has become real. In fact, that is what I would be confirming to you if I were to give you this formula. I would be conveying a meaning to you that is inconsistent with truth.

I will give you a hint. What you will find when you have Awakened, is that you have never stopped being totally Loving, that you never have seen an expression from any aspect of God's Creation which could bring you a message that was not loving. So as you look for things to allow to pass away, my suggestion would be this: let go of those things that come to your perception as not being loving and not being representative of, or consistent with, your recognizing who you Are. I will further define those things as being sensations of fear. Categorically, I will say give up your belief in fear and there will be nothing left that seems to contradict Love. As you give up the belief in fear, as you adopt the meaning that is inherent in being defenseless, you are acknowledging to yourself that your safety lies solely in expressing the Loving Being that you Are.

Much of the time you will expect more from my answers than what I may give you because they will appear to be too simple. You will say to yourself, "It must be more involved than this." But I will say to you, as you allow yourself to hear the Voice of simplicity, you will know you are hearing Truth.

Appendix

Appendix

Where Jesus Found God

"Never before had we realized there was an alternative to what we had perceived as truth."

Jesus' Revelation and Discovery of the Holy Spirit

Always curious as to how Jesus' awakening had unfolded here on earth, I asked how this had occurred. The answer was very interesting. It helped me to understand why his *A Course in Miracles* is written the way it is, as well as making my own awakening process more focused. Few are aware of the great shift in consciousness that Jesus actually brought into awareness at that time and continues to do so today.

He said that from his mid-teens he had been drawn to follow a yearning he could not clearly describe at the time, but somehow he knew would determine the course of his life. By his early twenties he was spending as much time as possible listening to discussions at the synagogue. Listening to the elders as they spoke of God touched him deeply, but discussions of their religious doctrines left him troubled, primarily because he could not accept their conflicting images of a God said to be compassionate and loving but Who demanded strict adherence to "laws" that were hardly compassionate or loving.

The meeting places for worship was also where travelers passing through the villages met to bring news of the world. It was here he first heard of a gathering place in what we now know as India, where seekers of all religious backgrounds came together to exchange ideas and insights. He was drawn to find this place, and when a passing traveler said he knew of the village, would be going in that direction, and invited him to come, he quickly decided to go.

His time there was most rewarding. He found it interesting to hear of other religious and philosophic beliefs, with both similar and contrasting ideas to his own religion. The major topics discussed dealt with the desire to reduce hunger and oppression and find a basis for peace in the world. But of most interest were the discussions regarding the brotherhood of man. There were many who shared his own belief of the connectedness of all life, but he was still left with his basic dilemma: If God created the world, which was the accepted belief, and if He was all loving, why could he find no evidence of that in the world?

He spent nearly a year on his journey as he explored the many places and different cultures he had heard others speak of. He would frequently stop and speak with those who were interested in the compassionate and loving God he believed in. Yet wherever he went, he could find no real evidence of an only loving God in the world of pain God was thought to have made. There were no illustrations of a brotherhood of man, of good rising above evil, or even of love being preferred to hate. If there was a brotherhood, an oneness of man, why did it seem our basic nature to pull apart and attack one another? He somehow knew the answer to this was key to his life's purpose, and so it became the focus of his seeking to know.

Determined to find an answer, after returning home he went to his favorite meditation place beside a small stream in the nearby hills. There were key issues he needed to resolve: (1) Is the creator God, as he believed, only kind and loving; (2) Is there a brotherhood, a oneness of man, and, (3) If there is truth in a loving harmony amongst all creation, why is there no evidence of it in the world? It was as he focused on these issues which his perception could not fathom that he first broke through the boundary of that perception and became aware of a Presence within his mind; a source of knowing unrelated to anything he had experienced before. He "heard" an inner Voice say to him that his perception of a loving God was correct, but he was looking for Him in the wrong places.

What was revealed to him then was to be the beginning of an unfolding awareness that would continue for the rest of his earthly experience. Each of his questions would be answered as he brought them to the light of this truth he had opened to, much in the same fashion he now teaches us through the forgiveness process in *A Course in Miracles*. As he came to know the nature of his mind as part of the one Mind, he knew there was nothing he could not know. He also strongly felt that God had given him this revelation as answer to his confusion, and found great comfort resting in the trust and peace of the Presence he now felt to be a part of him.

From the moment he first became aware of that inner guidance, he began to experience a flow of awareness he recognized was too different to be in any way reconcilable with what he had previously known. The more he absorbed, the clearer it became there was simply no way his perception could have brought this to him. He quickly came to understand he had finally accessed a connection to the loving God he had sought.

As he returned to the familiarity of the physical world, it became starkly obvious there was no way to reconcile his prior state of mind to what he now perceived. They were, he immediately knew, opposite in all respects, too different for one to ever lead to the other. His revelation was that truth must always point to or directly express oneness, while everything in the world of perception derives it's meaning from how it is different from something else. This made plain to him the direction his path must now take. As he saw this as his direction, he came to associate the source of his new-found knowing with the Presence he first called the "Gift of God", and later the "Voice for God". He was told that God had placed this Gift in mind for the very purpose of providing the alternative we needed to remember the truth, which our perception cannot access.

With this understanding, it was easier to see why there seemed to be so much suffering and injustice. The people were literally doing it to themselves. He could see, however, that changing an entire way of thinking was going to be difficult. What he had discovered was a way of thinking that was radically different from the traditional way of thinking and would likely require some radically different ways of teaching. It became increasingly obvious that the perceptions of the ego world's thinking had caused the world's problems, but could not solve them.

It was at this time he also became aware of a significant dilemma: the purpose of bringing this new awareness to the world was far greater than to simply solve the world's problems. The world, of course, as yet had no awareness of what he had come to know. Healing bodies and correcting injustice were the problems they wanted and needed to have addressed. How, he wondered, was he to deal with meeting their needs to fix the problems of the world while also freeing them to heal the beliefs, which were the source of their real "problems?"

Taking this issue to his new-found Guidance, he quickly discovered an added dimension: God's Answer to our misperceived separation was complete; there must be within each of us both the awareness of truth to correct our misperceptions, and the awareness of how to use it to achieve its end. Means and end together, what to do and how to do it joined through the Holy Spirit. What we are now studying in A Course in Miracles is an explanation of what this truth is and how we reevaluate our perception to the moment of relinquishing it.

Few of us really understand the great shift in awareness that Jesus' revelation brought into consciousness. This beautifully loving teacher accessed a completely different, totally harmonious state of mind underlying the dualistic, conflicted ego perception. Never before had we realized there was an alternative to what we had perceived as truth. Not a way to change or purify what we had perceived, but what literally was a different way to perceive ourselves. And one that would deny all the body's eyes seemed to see. It was how and where God can be experienced.

Appendix

About Tom and Linda

"Ask and you shall receive' is real."

About Tom and Linda

After a normal life in which both Tom and I eventually helped raise four children plus two wonderful young teenage boys from Vietnam who joined our family in 1979, and after experiencing the ups and downs of Tom's independent business experiences, we found ourselves with what the world might value as a degree of material success. While very enjoyable, we both felt that there must be more meaning to this life than that focus, and we began a search for greater understanding of what that purpose might be. After our children were successfully on their own, we felt inspired to move to an environment with less material focus than the suburban lifestyle. Therefore, in 1985 we left the Denver area and chose to live on the beautiful island of Kauai in Hawaii.

While still in Denver, in 1977 a new book called *A Course In Miracles* had been given us. Although initially neither of us could hardly understand anything in those pages, I persisted in trying to understand what was offered because of an inner feeling that these were indeed, Holy words. After moving to Kauai and after building a new home for two years, we both finally had time to focus on exploring this extraordinary teaching and eventually invited a few friends to join with us. That discussion group grew larger and in 1989 Tom silently made a deal with the Holy Spirit, not even sure such a Spirit existed: if this Holy Spirit would care to help him understand the *Course* more clearly, Tom said he would be willing to share that understanding with others.

Much to his surprise, within a few weeks, he began to hear an inner voice that answered every question of any nature that arose in his thoughts. He wondered if he was actually losing his mind as "channeling" as it was then called, was not something he was aware of. However, when he shared some of the information he heard with me, I somehow recognized the purity of the words and encouraged him to allow it to unfold. It wasn't long before we realized that this was indeed coming from somewhere beyond the worldly focus, and were rather amazed when the identity was acknowledged "as one you would recognize as once having been known as Jesus."

We were a bit awed and yet, at the same time, this seemed to be a familiar presence, especially to Tom who immediately felt comfortable calling this source, "Brother."

Of course we wondered why we were having this experience when so many people have spent lifetimes praying for such a thing. The answer from Brother was that this was a mutual choice. In hindsight, I have realized that we had first, asked for help, and second, were of a state of mind that could hear what was being offered. Neither of us had been satisfied with answers of the religions we had experienced in our past, and so our mind was not closed by a particular belief system. In other words, we were open, reasonably intelligent and well-balanced, and were not so overwhelmed by the identity of the source as to distort his purpose.

Initially, I began recording questions which I and a few close friends would ask of Brother through Tom. The information was so beautiful and I wanted to be able to go over it again and again. I began to transcribe the tapes on a new thing called a "computer" and soon these printed transcriptions began to be passed on to others who also were interested in receiving copies. A few years later, we put together most of those transcriptions into the form you have just read and called it, *Dialogue on Awakening,* which we first published in 1992. (In subsequent printings, we have added a few timely questions and answers.)

It wasn't long before Jesus suggested that Tom let go of the idea that he was "channeling" and to recognize that the Source of all knowledge was as much available to him and everyone else as it was to Jesus. Tom was willing to try to do this and soon was able to access that wondrous place of awareness within his mind where all minds are One and to share what he could with others when asked. Yet the relationship with Brother to this day remains as our friend, our teacher, and the example of who we and you Are in truth.

We both will eternally cherish this beloved Being who always seems to be "on call" with inspiration, guidance, humor, and what seems to be to be infinite patience with our ignorance and many faults. We are always glad to share our growing awareness with others when asked, but both of us are clear that our primary focus is our own journey of remembering the truth of who we are. If what you have read in these pages has helped you to do the same, then we are most grateful to have been of some help to you.

"Ask and you shall receive" is real.

I hope this information will give you, as it has given me, an expansion into more joy, more peace and harmony, and of course, a greater acceptance of Love's Presence—the essence of who we are now and forever must Be. These words are a tool, not a stopping place, for infinite Love has no absolute definitions, no boundaries or limitations.